BETTER ENGLISH PRONUNCIATION

Better English Pronunciation

J. D. O'Connor

Reader in Phonetics in the
University of London

Cambridge University Press

Cambridge
London · New York · Melbourne

Published by the Syndics of the Cambridge University Press
The Pitt Building, Trumpington Street, Cambridge CB2 IRP
Bentley House, 200 Euston Road, London NWI 2DB
32 East 57th Street, New York, NY 10022, USA
296 Beaconsfield Parade, Middle Park, Melbourne 3206, Australia

Library of Congress catalogue card number: 67–10151

ISBN 0 521 09415 1 paperback
ISBN 0 521 05859 7 hard covers

First published 1967
Reprinted 1970 1971 1972 1975 1976 1977 (twice) 1979

Printed in Great Britain at the
University Press, Cambridge

CONTENTS

CONTENTS

ACKNOWLEDGEMENTS

Every writer of a textbook owes a debt to his predecessors, to his teachers, to his colleagues and to his pupils; I gratefully acknowledge my deep indebtedness to all of these. In addition I wish to express particular thanks to Mrs M. Chan of Hongkong, Miss Afaf M. E. Elmenoufi of Cairo and Dr R. K. Bansal of Hyderabad for very kindly helping me with regard to the pronunciation difficulties of Cantonese, Arabic and Hindi speakers respectively. Last, but far from least, my very sincere thanks go to my friends Pauline Speller, who typed the whole of a by no means easy manuscript and did it admirably, and Dennis Speller, who drew for me exactly the illustrations that I wanted and could not have done for myself.

The responsibility for the book is mine; any credit I happily share with all those mentioned above.

University College London   J. D. O'C.

1

PROBLEMS IN PRONUNCIATION

The purpose of this book is very simple: to help you, the reader, to pronounce English better than you do now. Millions of foreign students want to learn English as well as they can; for some it is only a matter of reading and writing it, and they will find no help here. But many students want to be able to speak English well, with a pronunciation which can be easily understood both by their fellow-students and by English people, and it is for them that this book is specially intended.

Written English and spoken English are obviously very different things. Writing consists of marks on paper which make no noise and are taken in by the eye, whilst speaking is organized sound, taken in by the ear. How can a book, which is nothing but marks on paper, help anyone to make their English *sound* better? The answer to this is that it can't, not by itself. But if you will co-operate, and listen to English as much as you can, along the lines that I shall suggest to you, then you will find that the instructions given in the following pages will make your ears sharper for the sound of English and when you can *hear* English properly you can go on and improve your performance.

Language starts with the ear. When a baby starts to talk he does it by hearing the sounds his mother makes and imitating them. If a baby is born deaf he cannot hear these sounds and therefore cannot imitate them and will not speak. But normal babies can hear and can imitate; they are wonderful imitators, and this gift of imitation, which gives us the gift of speech, lasts for a number of years. It is well known that a child of ten years old or less can learn *any* language perfectly, if it is brought up surrounded by that language, no matter where it was born or who its parents were. But after this age the ability to imitate perfectly becomes less, and we all know only too well that adults have great difficulty in mastering the pronunciation (as well as other parts) of foreign languages. Some people are more talented than others; they find pronouncing other languages less difficult, but they never find them easy. Why is this? Why should this gift that we all have as children disappear in later life? Why can't grown-up people pick up the characteristic sound of a foreign language as a child can?

The answer to this is that our native language won't let us. By the time we are grown up the habits of our own language are so strong that they are very difficult to break. In our own language we have a fairly small number of sound-units which we put together in many different combinations to form the words and sentences we use every day. And as we get older we are dominated by this small number of units. It is as if we had in our heads a certain fixed number of boxes for sounds; when we listen to our own language we hear the sounds and we put each into the right box, and when we speak we go to the boxes and take out the sounds we want in the order we want them. And as we do this over the years the boxes get stronger and stronger until everything we hear, whether it is our own language or another, has to be put into one of these boxes, and everything we say comes out of one of them. But every language has a different number of boxes, and the boxes are arranged differently. For example, three of our English boxes contain the sounds at the beginning of the words *fin*, *thin* and *sin*, that is, *f*, *th* (this is one sound, of course) and *s*. Like this:

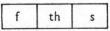

Now, many other languages have boxes which are similar to the English ones for *f* and *s*, but they do not have a special box for the *th*-sound. And we can picture this in the following way:

f	th	s
f		s

When the foreign listener hears the English *th*-sound he has to put it in one of his own boxes, his habits force him to do so, and he has no special *th* box, so he puts it into either the *f* box or the *s* box:

f	th	s
f		s

In other words, he 'hears' the *th*-sound as either *f* or *s*; a funny *f* or a funny *s*, no doubt, but he has nowhere else to put it. And in speaking the same thing happens: if he has to say *thin*, he has no *th* box to go to so he goes to the nearest box available to him, either the *f* or the *s*, and he says either *fin* or *sin*.

The main problem of English pronunciation is to build a new set of boxes corresponding to the sounds of English, and to break down the arrangement of boxes which the habits of our native language has so strongly built up. We do this by establishing new ways of hearing, new ways of using our speech organs, new speech habits.

This may sound easy, but it isn't. Unfortunately, it is never easy to establish good habits, it is always the bad ones which come most naturally, and you will need to do a great deal of hard work if you want to build yourself a set of English boxes which are nearly as firm as those of your own language. Anyone who says that you can get a good English pronunciation without hard work is talking rubbish, unless you happen to be one of the very small number of lucky people to whom pronunciation comes fairly easily. Most of us need to work hard at it, and this book is for people who are prepared to work hard. If you work hard and regularly along the lines suggested in this book, you will improve. One of the most important things to remember is that *everyone can improve*, even if they have no great talent for language. Quite apart from anything else, there is great satisfaction to be got from the development of what talent you have. You may never sound like a native English speaker, but at least you will have got as close to it as you can.

'LEND ME YOUR EARS'

If speech depends on hearing, and books don't talk, what are you to do? Fortunately there is a lot of English spoken about the world. On films, on the radio, on gramophone records; most people can get the opportunity of listening to English in some way, and this is what you must do. *You must hear English.* But just hearing it is not enough; you must listen to it, and you must listen to it not for the meaning but for the sound of it. Obviously when you are listening to a radio programme you will be trying to understand it, trying to get the meaning from it; but you must try also for at least a short part of the time to forget about what the words mean and to listen to them simply as sounds. Take one of the English sounds at a time, it might be the English *t*, and listen for it each time it comes; concentrate on catching it, on picking it out, on hearing what it sounds like. Don't just be satisfied to hear it vaguely, as if it were a sound of your own language; try and pick out the Englishness of it, what makes it different from the nearest sound in your language. And when you think you have got it, then say it in some of the words that you have heard,

4

and say it *aloud*. It is no use practising silently; all of us are much better at pronouncing if we do it silently, inside ourselves. But you can't talk English inside yourself, it has to come out, so practice aloud, even if it puzzles your family or your friends. Later in the book you will find pronunciation exercises to be done; these too must be done aloud.

Films or radio programmes have the disadvantage that you can't stop them and ask for something to be repeated. Gramophone records do not have this disadvantage. With gramophone records you can repeat any part of the text as often as you need, and you must do this: it is much better for your ear if you listen to the same passage six times than if you listen to six different passages; but be careful—listen closely each time, don't relax after two or three hearings, try to keep your ears as closely concentrated on the sound of the passage at the sixth hearing as at the first. In this way you will build up a store of sound-memory which will form a firm base for your performance.

Now, performance. When you practise (aloud, of course), you must still listen carefully and accurately. If you have listened properly in the first place you will know what the English words and sentences sound like, and you must compare as closely as you can the sounds that come out of your mouth with the sounds that you are holding in your head, in your sound-memory. Don't be satisfied too easily, try to match your sounds exactly with the sounds that you have listened to.

Some of you may be able to make use of a tape-recorder; if you can, you will be able to hear what you sound like to other people and this is very helpful. If you can, record on the tape-recorder a sentence or a longer passage with which you are familiar through hearing it said by an English speaker. Then listen to it, closely and carefully, and see where your performance does not match the original;

mark the places where you are dissatisfied, and practise these bits until you think you have them right; then re-record the passage, listen critically again, and repeat the sequence. One word of warning—a tape-recorder will not do the job for you; it is a useful instrument, but it is not a magic wand which will make your English perfect without any effort from you. It is useful only because it enables you to listen to yourself from the outside, which makes it easier for you to hear what is wrong, but it is you who have to put it right, and the machine cannot do this for you. In the end it is absolutely essential for you to be able to match what you say with your sound-memory of English. So although a tape-recorder is helpful, this does not mean that if you haven't got one your English will not improve, and, just as important, it does not mean that if you have a tape-recorder your English will necessarily be better. Careful listening is the most important thing; and careful matching of performance with listening will bring you nearer to the ideal of a perfect English pronunciation. And make no mistake, your aim must be to acquire a perfect English pronunciation. You will almost certainly not succeed in this aim because it requires, as I have said, a very rare gift; but unless this is your aim you will not make all the progress of which you are capable; keep working towards perfection until you are quite sure that it is neither necessary nor profitable for you to continue. Then you will have done yourself justice.

WHICH ENGLISH?

What do we mean by a perfect English pronunciation? In one sense there are as many different kinds of English as there are speakers of it; no two people speak exactly alike—we can always hear differences between them—and the pronunciation of English varies a great deal in different geographical areas. How do we decide what sort of English to use as a model? This is not a question which can be decided in the same way for all foreign learners of English. If you live in a part of the world like India or West Africa, where there is a tradition of speaking English for general communication purposes, you should aim to acquire a good variety of the pronunciation of this area; such varieties of Indian English or African English and the like are to be respected and used as a model by all those who will need their English mainly for the purpose of communication with their fellows in these areas. It would be a mistake in these circumstances to use as a model B.B.C. English or anything of the sort.

On the other hand, if you live in an area where there is no traditional use of English and no body of people who speak it for general communication purposes, then you must take as your model some form of native English pronunciation, and which form you choose does not very much matter. The most sensible thing to do is to take as your model the sort of English which you can hear most often. If you have gramophone records of English speech based on, let us say, an American pronunciation, make American your model; if you can listen regularly to the B.B.C., use that kind of English. But whatever you choose to do, remember this: all these different accents of English have a great deal in common, they have far more similarities than differences, so don't worry too much what sort of English you are listening to provided it *is* English.

In this book I cannot describe all the possible pronunciations of English that might be useful to you so I shall concentrate on one, the sort of English used by educated native speakers in south-east England, often referred to as Received Pronunciation (R.P. for short), that is 'accepted' pronunciation. R.P. will be the basis; but I am less interested in making you speak with this particular accent of

English than in helping you to make the necessary differences between the basic sounds which are found in all kinds of English: these are found in R.P. and because of this it is as useful to describe R.P. as to describe any other native pronunciation, and if you really want to speak with a British accent, then this is as good as any, in the sense that it is widely acceptable.

THE BASIC SOUNDS

The sounds at the beginning of each of the words in the following list are all different: the letters which stand for these sounds (usually one letter per sound, but sometimes two) are printed in italic type:

*p*ier	*v*eer	*n*ear
*b*eer	*sh*eer	*w*eir
*t*ier	*h*ear	*y*ear
*d*eer	*l*eer	*ch*eer
*g*ear	*r*ear	*j*eer
*f*ear	*m*ere	

It is the sound at the beginning of the word, the initial sound, which makes one word different from all the other words in the list. Since this is so, since these sounds are *distinctive*, it is obviously necessary to be able to make them sound different: they are basic sounds of English—all kinds of English. So are the sounds of the letters in italic type in these lists:

ba*se*	wra*th*
bai*ze*	wro*ng*
ba*the*	
bei*ge*	
ba*ke*	

In these lists the sounds at the end of the word are distinctive, the final sounds. If you count up the sounds which are distinctive in initial and final position you will find that there are twenty-four altogether. And these twenty-four sounds which occur initially and finally, though they occur in other positions too, are called *consonants*.

Now look at these lists:

f*ee*l	c*a*t	p*ie*r
f*i*ll	c*o*t	p*ea*r
f*e*ll	c*u*t	p*oo*r
f*a*ll	c*ur*t	
f*u*ll	c*ar*t	
f*oo*l		
f*ai*l		
f*oa*l		
f*i*le		
f*ou*l		
f*oi*l		

Most of these sounds, represented again by letters in italic type, occur surrounded by consonants, and this is typical, although most of them can also occur initially and finally too. These sounds are called *vowels*.

Notice. 1. Five of these words, *curt, cart, pier, pear, poor*, have a letter *r* in them. In many English accents, e.g. American, Canadian, Scottish, Irish, this would be pronounced exactly like the consonant at the beginning of *red*, but in R.P. and various other accents the letter represents part of a basic vowel unit. There is more detail about this on p. 79.

2. There is one other vowel, making twenty in all, which occurs in the word b*a*nan*a*. This is a very special and very important vowel in English and it is discussed in full on pp. 105–7.

LETTERS AND SOUNDS

These must never be mixed up. Letters are written, sounds are spoken. It is very useful to have written letters to remind us of corresponding sounds, but this is all they do; they cannot make us pronounce sounds which we do not already know; they simply remind us. In ordinary English spelling it is not always easy to know what sounds the letters stand for; for example, in the words *city, busy, women, pretty, village,* the letters *i, y, u, o, e* and *a* all stand for the *same* vowel sound, the one which occurs in *sit.* And in *banana, bather, man, many* the letter *a* stands for five different vowel sounds. In a book which is dealing with pronunciation this is inconvenient; it would be much more useful if the reader could always be certain that one letter represented one and only one sound, that when he saw a letter he would know at once how to pronounce it (or at least what to aim at!). That is why it is helpful to use letters in a consistent way when dealing with English. We have twenty-four consonants and twenty vowels to consider and we give to each of these forty-four units a letter (or sometimes two letters, if this is convenient). In that way we can show without any doubt what the student should be trying to say.

Here again are the words listed on p. 8, and this time beside each word is the letter of the International Phonetic Alphabet which will *always* be used to represent the sound to which that word is the key, however it may be spelt in other words. Most of the letters will be perfectly familiar to you, others will seem strange for a little while; but not for long.

*p*ier /p/	*f*ear /f/	*r*ear /r/	*ch*eer /tʃ/
*b*eer /b/	*v*eer /v/	*m*ere /m/	*j*eer /dʒ/
*t*ier /t/	*sh*eer /ʃ/	*n*ear /n/	
*d*eer /d/	*h*ear /h/	*w*eir /w/	
*g*ear /g/	*l*eer /l/	*y*ear /j/	

ba*se* /s/	wra*th* /θ/		
bai*ze* /z/	wro*ng* /ŋ/		
ba*the* /ð/			
bei*ge* /ʒ/			
ba*ke* /k/			

f*ee*l /iː/	f*ai*l /ei/	c*a*t /æ/	p*ie*r /iə/
f*i*ll /i/	f*oa*l /ou/	c*o*t /ɔ/	p*ea*r /ɛə/
f*e*ll /e/	f*i*le /ai/	c*u*t /ʌ/	p*oo*r /uə/
f*a*ll /ɔː/	f*ou*l /au/	c*u*rt /əː/	
f*u*ll /u/	f*oi*l /ɔi/	c*a*rt /ɑː/	b*a*nan*a* /ə/
f*oo*l /uː/			

The use of the colon (ː) with the vowels /iː, ɔː, uː, əː/ is to show that they are in general *longer* than /i, ɔ, u, ə/. They are also different in their actual sound, though this is not shown separately. The vowel /ɑː/ is also one of the longer vowels.

Here are some examples of words written in this way: *city* siti, *busy* bizi, *women* wimin, *banana* bənɑːnə, *bather* beiðə, *man* mæn, *many* meni, *wrong* rɔŋ, *change* tʃeindʒ, *house* haus, *thought* θɔːt, *could* kud, *cough* kɔf, *rough* rʌf, *though* ðou.

This way of writing or transcribing makes it possible to show that some words which are ordinarily spelt in the same way sound different; for example, *lead*, which is pronounced liːd in a phrase like *lead the way*, but led in *lead pipe*. It also makes clear that some words which are spelt differently sound the same, for example, *rain*, *rein*, *reign*, which are all pronounced rein.

SOUNDS AND SOUND-GROUPS

A sound is made by definite movements of the organs of speech, and if those movements are exactly repeated the result will always be the same sound; it is easy to show that there are more than forty-four sounds in English—even in the pronunciation of a single person, without worrying about differences between people. For instance, if you say *tea* and *two* tiː, tuː you will notice that the lips are in a rather flat shape for tiː but are made rounder for tuː, and this is true for both the consonant /t/ and for the two vowels. So the organs of speech are not making *exactly* the same movements for the /t/ of *tea* and the /t/ of *two*, and therefore the resulting sounds are not exactly the same. You can prove this to yourself by only saying the consonant sounds of these words: think of the word *tea* and pronounce the beginning of it—but not the vowel. Then do the same for *two*; think of the word but stop before the vowel: you can hear and feel that the two sounds are different. Obviously most of the movements we make when pronouncing these two sounds are the same, and they therefore sound alike, but not identical.

Take another example, /h/. When we pronounce the words *he*, *hat*, *who* hiː, hæt, huː, the h-sounds are different: in pronouncing /h/ we put our mouth into the position needed for the following vowel and then push out air through this position, but since the three different vowels have three different mouth-positions it follows that the three h-sounds must also be different. You can prove this again, as with the t-sounds, by saying the beginnings of these words whilst only thinking the rest.

Each of the letters we use to show pronunciation may stand for more than one sound; but each of the sounds represented by one letter has a great deal of similarity to the other sounds represented by the same letter; they have more similarities than differences: none of the h-sounds could be mistaken for an l- or an s-sound, and none of the t-sounds can be confused with a p- or a k-sound.

These groups of sounds, each represented by one letter of the phonetic alphabet, are called *phonemes*, and the method of representing each phoneme by one symbol is called *phonemic transcription*. Phonemic transcription may be enclosed in diagonal lines /........./. It is necessary to distinguish carefully between phonemes and sounds: the 44 phonemes of English are the basic contrasts which make it possible for us to keep each word or longer utterance separate from every other, fiːl from fil and piə from biə, etc. But each phoneme may be represented by different sounds in different positions, so the different t-sounds in *tea* and *two* both represent the /t/ phoneme, and the three h-sounds in *he, hat, who* all represent the single /h/ phoneme.

This suggests two stages in the learning of pronunciation: the first is to be able to produce 44 vowels and consonants which are different, so that the words and longer utterances of English do not at any rate sound the same, so that fiːl and fil sound different. At this stage the learner will not worry about which of the possible h-sounds he is using; any of them will serve to distinguish *heat* hiːt from *eat* iːt. The common feature of each phoneme is reproduced, all the necessary distinctions of words, etc., can be made. But obviously if the learner uses a particular sound in a word where an English speaker uses a different sound belonging to the same phoneme, the effect will be odd; he will not be misunderstood—that could only happen if he used a sound belonging to a different phoneme—but he will not be performing in an English way, and if this happens with many of the phonemes it will contribute to a foreign accent. So the second stage in learning pronunciation must be to learn to use as many different sounds as is necessary to represent a particular phoneme. In theory a single phoneme is represented by a different sound in every different position in which it occurs, but most of these differences will be made automatically by the learner without instruction. It is only in cases where this is un-likely to happen that it will be necessary to worry about particular sounds within a phoneme.

There is one other relation between sound and phoneme which is likely to give trouble. Here is an example: in English /d/ and /ð/ are different phonemes; in Spanish there are sounds which are similar to those used in English to represent these phonemes—we can write them d and ð; but in Spanish these two sounds belong to the *same* phoneme—when the phoneme occurs between vowels it is represented by ð, as in *nada* 'nothing', but when it occurs in initial position it is represented by d, as in *dos* 'two'. This will cause difficulty for the Spanish speaker because although he has more or less the same sounds as in English he is not able to use them independently, and whenever an English /d/ occurs between vowels he will be in danger of using /ð/, and confusing *breeding* briːdiŋ with *breathing* briːðiŋ, and whenever English /ð/ occurs in initial position he will be in danger of using /d/, and confusing *they* ðei and *day* dei. In general, if two sounds belong to one phoneme in your language, but to two different phonemes in English there will be danger of confusions until you have learnt to forget the habits of your language and use the sounds independently as in English. This can be done by careful listening and accurate use of the speech organs and a great deal of practice.

WORDS AND UTTERANCES

Most of what I have said so far has been about the pro-nunciation of short pieces of speech, sounds or single words; it is necessary at first to be sure that the basic sounds of the language are being properly pronounced and the best way of doing that is to practise single words or very short phrases; but we do not talk in single words, and certainly not in single sounds. The sounds and words are connected together with others to make up longer utterances, and these longer utterances have special difficulties of their own.

First, they must be pronounced smoothly, without hesitations and without stumbling over the combinations of sounds. It may be quite easy to pronounce separately the words, *library, been, lately, you, to, the, have,* but it is much more difficult to pronounce the question *Have you been to the library lately?* without hesitating and without making mistakes.

Secondly, in a longer English utterance some of the words are treated as being more important to the meaning than others, and it is necessary to know which these words are and how they are treated in speech. And words which are not regarded as being particularly important often have a different pronunciation because of this; for example, the word *can* which is pronounced kæn if it is said by itself, is often pronounced kən in phrases like *You can have it* ju: kən hæv it.

Thirdly, the rhythm of English must be mastered, that is, the different lengths which the syllables of English are given and the reasons why these different lengths occur. An example of this would be the following:

The c h a i r collapsed.

The chairman collapsed.

The word *chair* has the same length as the word *chairman,* and therefore the two syllables in *chairman* are shorter than the single syllable of *chair,* so that the *chair* of *chairman* is only half as long as the word *chair* by itself.

Fourthly, and last, the tune of the voice, the melody of speech is different in different languages and it is necessary to learn something of the English way of using tune. For example, when we say *thank you*, the voice may go from a higher note to a lower one, or it may go from a lower note to a higher one and these two different tunes show two different attitudes: higher to lower means sincere gratitude; lower to higher means that the matter is purely routine. To confuse the two would clearly be dangerous and it is necessary to learn what tunes there are in English and what they mean.

All these matters will be dealt with in the chapters which follow, and exercises will be given to help the reader to improve his performance at each stage. But the first important thing is to be sure that the basic sound-distinctions are right and this requires knowledge of the working of the speech organs; this is the subject of the second chapter.

EXERCISES ON CHAPTER I

(Answers on p. 163.)

1. How many *phonemes* are there in the following words (the lists on p. 10 will help you here)?: *write, through, measure, six, half, where, one, first, voice, castle, scissors, should, judge, father, lamb.*

2. *Bear* and *bare* are spelt differently but pronounced the same, bɛə. Make a list of other words which are spelt differently but pronounced in the same way.

3. Write the words in Exercise 1 above in *phonemic* transcription, and then memorize the forty-four symbols needed to transcribe English phonemically so that you can do it without looking at the lists. Now transcribe the following words phonemically: *mat, met, meet, mate, might, cot, cut, caught, lick, look, bird, board, load, loud, boys, bars, bears, sheer, sure, copper, green, charge, song, five, with, truth, yellow, pleasure, hallo.*

4. Try to make lists like those on p. 8 for your language,

and see how many phonemes it uses. For some languages this will be quite easy, for some it will be difficult; if you have difficulty in finding words which are different only in one phoneme, find words which are as similar as you can. An English example of this kind is *getting*, *cutting* (which shows that /g, k/ and /e, ʌ/ are different phonemes). What phonemes does the pair *mother*, *father* separate?

2

HOW THE SPEECH ORGANS WORK
IN ENGLISH

In all languages we speak with air from the lungs. We
draw it into the lungs quickly and we release it slowly and
then interfere with its passage in various ways and at
various places. Figure 1 is a diagram showing a side view
of the parts of the throat and mouth and nose which are
important to recognize for English.

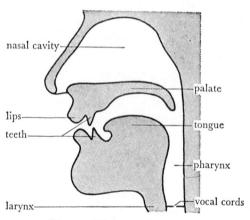

Fig. 1. The vocal organs.

THE VOCAL CORDS

The air released by the lungs comes up through the wind-
pipe and arrives first at *the larynx*. The larynx contains two
small bands of elastic tissue, which can be thought of as
two flat strips of rubber, lying opposite to each other
across the air passage.

The inner edges of the vocal cords can be moved towards each other so that they meet and completely cover the top of the wind-pipe, or they can be drawn apart so that there is a gap between them (known as the *glottis*) through which the air can pass freely: this is their usual position when we breathe quietly in and out.

When the vocal cords are brought together tightly no air can pass through them and if the lungs are pushing air

Fig. 2. The vocal cords.

from below this air is compressed. If the vocal cords are then opened suddenly the compressed air bursts out with a sort of coughing noise. Try this: open your mouth wide, hold your breath, imagine that you are picking up a heavy weight, holding it for two seconds, then dropping it and suddenly let your breath out. This holding back of the compressed air followed by a sudden release is called *the glottal stop*, and what you feel as the air bursts out is the vocal cords springing apart. Do this ten times, and get used to the feeling of the 'click' of the vocal cords as they release the air. The compression of the air may be very great, as when we do lift a heavy weight, or it may be quite slight, when the result is like a very gentle cough.

If the vocal cords are brought together quite gently, the air from the lungs will be able to force them apart for a moment, but then they will fall back together into the closed position; then the air will force them apart again, and they will close again, and so on. This is a very rapid process and may take place as many as 800 times per second. It is obviously not possible to hear each individual 'click' of the opening vocal cords, and what we do hear is a musical note. The height of the note depends on the speed of opening and closing of the vocal cords; if they open and close very quickly the note will be high, if they open and close slowly the note will be low. The note, whether high or low, produced by the rapid opening and closing of the vocal cords is called *voice*.

Some of the English sounds have voice and some do not. Say a long m-sound and put your fingers on your neck by the side of the larynx. You will feel the vibration of the vocal cords. Now keep your lips closed still, but just breathe hard through your nose: no vibration. Repeat this several times, first m then breath through the nose, and get used to the feeling of voice and no voice. Now say the word *more* mɔː, still with your fingers on your neck. Does the vowel /ɔː/ have voice? Can you still feel the same vibration for /ɔː/ as for /m/? Yes, both sounds are voiced. Say a long s-sound. Is it voiced? No, it has no vibrations. Try other sounds of your own language and English and see which of them are voiced and which not.

The sounds which are not voiced—*voiceless* sounds—are made with the vocal cords drawn apart so that the air can pass out freely between them and there is no vibration. The difference between voiced and voiceless can be used to distinguish between what are otherwise similar sounds. Say a long s-sound again, and in the middle of it turn the voice on: this will give you a z-sound, buzzing rather than hissing. But not all the voiced sounds of English have similar voiceless sounds, for example the voiceless m-sound which you made just now does not occur in English, and even when there are pairs of similar sounds which are voiced and voiceless this may not be the only difference between them, as we shall see later.

Immediately above the larynx is a space behind the tongue and reaching up towards the nasal cavity: this space is called the *pharynx* /færɪŋks/.

THE PALATE

The palate, as Figure 1 shows, forms the roof of the mouth and separates the mouth cavity from the nose (or nasal) cavity. Make the tip of your tongue touch as much of your own palate as you can: most of it is hard and fixed in position, but when your tongue-tip is as far back as it will go, away from your teeth, you will notice that the palate becomes soft. Figure 3 is a more detailed view of the palate.

You can easily see the soft part of the palate if you use a mirror: turn your back to the light, open your mouth wide

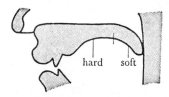

Fig. 3. The soft and hard parts of the palate.

and say the vowel /ɑː/, and move the mirror so that the light shines into your mouth. You will be able to see the soft palate curving down towards the tongue and becoming narrower as it does so until it ends in a point called the *uvula* /juːvjulə/. Behind the soft palate you will be able to see part of the back wall of the pharynx. The soft palate can move: it can be raised so that it makes a firm contact with the back wall of the pharynx (as in Figure 3), and this stops the breath from going up into the nasal cavity and forces it to go into the mouth only. You can see this raising of the soft palate in your mirror if you keep your mouth wide open in position for the vowel /ɑː/ and push out your breath very fast, as if you were trying to blow out a match, still with your mouth open wide. You will see the soft palate move quickly upwards so that the breath all comes out of the mouth and none of it goes up into the nasal cavity. And when you relax after this the soft palate will come down again into its lowered position, shown in Figure 4.

In this lowered position, the soft palate allows the breath to pass behind itself and up into the nasal cavity and out

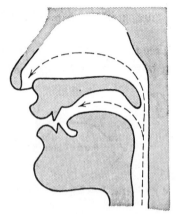

Fig. 4. The soft palate lowered.

through the nose, as the dotted line shows. This is the normal position of the soft palate when we are not speaking but breathing quietly through the nose, with our mouth closed. It is also the position for the m-, n- and ŋ-sounds; say a long m-sound and nip your nose; this will stop the breath moving, and when you release it, the breath will continue out in a normal m-sound. Keep your lips closed and blow breath (without voice) hard through your nose, then draw it in again sharply: this will give you the feeling of breath moving in and out behind the soft palate.

Now say a p but don't open your lips, just hold the breath behind the lips: there is no sound at all; keep your lips firmly closed still and send all the breath sharply out of the nose. Do this several times without opening your lips at all. What you feel at the back of your mouth is the soft palate going up and down; it is raised whilst you hold the p and lowered suddenly when you let the air rush out through your nose. For most of the sounds of all languages the soft palate is raised, so that the air is forced to go out through the mouth only.

Apart from this important raising and lowering of the soft palate, the whole of the palate, including the soft palate, is used by the tongue to interfere with the air stream. Say the vowel /ɑː/ again and watch the tongue in your mirror: it is flat in the mouth. Now add a k after the ɑː and you

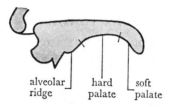

alveolar hard soft
ridge palate palate

Fig. 5. The parts of the palate.

will see the back part of your tongue rise up and touch the soft palate so that the breath is completely stopped; then when you lower your tongue the breath rushes out again.

The hard, fixed part of the palate is divided into two sections, shown in Figure 5, the *alveolar ridge* /ælvioulə ridʒ/ and the *hard palate*. The alveolar ridge is that part of the gums immediately behind the upper front teeth, and the hard palate is the highest part of the palate, between the alveolar ridge and the beginning of the soft palate. You can touch the whole of the alveolar ridge and the hard palate with your tongue-tip. The alveolar ridge is especially important in English because many of the consonant sounds like /t d n l r s z ʃ ʒ tʃ dʒ/ are made with the tongue touching or close to the alveolar ridge.

Finally the palate curves downwards towards the teeth at each side.

THE TEETH

The lower front teeth are not important in speech except that if they are missing certain sounds, e.g. s and z, will be difficult to make. But the two upper front teeth are used in English to some extent. Put the tip of your tongue very close to the edge of these teeth and blow: this will produce a sound like the English θ in *thin*; if you turn on the voice during this θ-sound you will get a sound like the English ð in *this*.

THE TONGUE

The tongue is the most important of the organs of speech because it has the greatest variety of movement. Although the tongue has no obvious natural divisions like the palate,

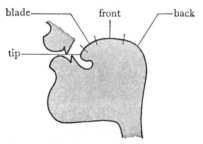

Fig. 6. The parts of the tongue.

it is useful to think of it as divided into four parts, as shown in Figure 6.

The *back* of the tongue lies under the soft palate when the tongue is at rest; the *front* lies under the hard palate, the *tip* and the *blade* lie under the alveolar ridge, the tip being the most forward part of all and the blade between the tip and the front. The tip and blade are particularly mobile and, as we have seen, they can touch the whole of the lips, the teeth, the alveolar ridge and the hard palate. The front can be flat on the bottom of the mouth or it can be raised to touch the hard palate, or it can be raised to any extent between these two extremes. Say the vowel /ɑː/ again and look into your mirror: the front is flat on the

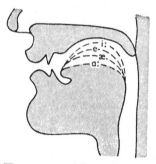

Fig. 7. Tongue positions for /iː, e, æ, ɑː/

bottom of the mouth; now say /æ/ as in *cat*: the front rises a little; now say /e/ as in *met* (still keep your mouth as wide open as you can): the front rises again; and if you go on to say /iː/ as in *see* you will see that the front rises to a very high position, so high that it is hidden behind the teeth. These positions are shown in Figure 7. For /iː/ the front of the tongue comes very close to the hard palate. Put your mouth in this position, for /iː/, and draw air *inwards* quickly; you will feel cold air on the front of the tongue and on the hard palate just above it.

The back of the tongue too can be flat in the mouth, or it can be raised to touch the soft palate, or it can be raised to any position between these two extremes. Say /ɑːk/ again, as you did earlier, and hold the k-sound with your mouth wide open. You will see in your mirror that the back of the tongue rises from a very flat position for ɑː to a position actually touching the soft palate for the k. Figure 8 shows these two extreme positions. The back of the tongue is in various positions between these two ex-

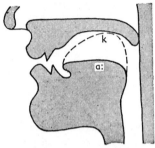

Fig. 8. Tongue positions for /ɑː, k/.

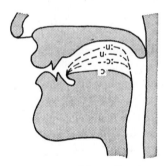

Fig. 9. Tongue positions for /uː, u, ɔː, ɔ/.

tremes for the vowels /ɔ, ɔː, u, uː/; say them in that order and feel the back of the tongue rise gradually towards the soft palate: you will not be able to see the movement in the mirror because the lips will be in the way, but the position of the back of the tongue for each of these vowels is shown in Figure 9. In uː the back of the tongue is very close to the soft palate; put your mouth in position for uː and draw air *inwards* quickly: you will feel cold air on the back of the tongue and the soft palate. Now do the same for i: again and feel the difference when the front of the tongue is raised. Go from the i: position to the u: position several times whilst drawing breath inwards, and get used to this difference between a high front and a high back position.

The tongue can also change its shape in another way. Say the sound s, keep your mouth in the s position and draw breath inwards; you will feel cold air passing through

Fig. 10. Front view of flat tongue.

Fig. 11. Front view of grooved tongue.

a narrow passage between the blade of the tongue and the alveolar ridge, but no cold air at the sides of the tongue. Now say an l-sound and draw air inwards. This time you will feel cold air passing between the *sides* of the tongue and the sides of the palate, but not down the centre of the tongue. This is because for s the sides of the tongue are pressed firmly against the sides of the palate, so that the breath is forced to pass down the narrow central passage between the blade of the tongue and the alveolar ridge. In l the centre of the mouth is blocked by the tip and blade of the tongue pressed firmly against the alveolar ridge and the air passes instead between the sides of the tongue and the sides of the palate. So the sides of the tongue may be either curved upwards to meet the sides of the palate or left flat so that they do not touch the sides of the palate. Open your mouth wide, use your mirror and try to make your tongue take up a flat shape, as in Figure 10, and then a curved shape, with the sides raised but the centre line lower, as in Figure 11. This last position is very important for English because many of the consonant sounds are pronounced with the sides of the tongue curved up in this way to meet the sides of the palate.

THE LIPS

It is obvious that the lips can take up various different positions. They can be brought firmly together as in p or b or m so that they completely block the mouth; the lower lip can be drawn inward and slightly upwards to touch the upper front teeth as in the sounds f and v. And they can be kept apart either flat or with different amounts of rounding, and they can be pushed forward to a greater or lesser extent.

Of course, the closed position for p, b, m and the lip-teeth position for f and v are used in English, but apart from this the English do not move their lips with very much energy: their lips are never very far apart, they do not take up very rounded shapes, they are rarely spread very much and almost never pushed forward or protruded. Watch English people talk either in real life or on films and notice how little the lips and the lower jaw move; some people make more lip-movement than others, but it is never necessary to exaggerate these movements. Watch people talking your language too, and see whether they move their lips more than the English. If so, you must remember when talking English to use your lips less than you do in your own language. The same is true for movements of the jaw: in normal speech there is rarely more than half an inch between the lips or a quarter of an inch between the teeth even when the mouth is at its widest open. No wonder English can be spoken quite easily whilst holding a pipe between the teeth!

In the chapters which follow we shall see how the movements of the organs of speech combine together in forming the sounds of English. You should study the descriptions of the movements very carefully, because what seems a quite small difference may in fact be very important in producing and recognizing an English sound correctly, and the difference between an English sound and one in your language may seem quite small when it is described, but the small difference in the movement of the speech organs may make all the difference between a result which sounds English and one which does not.

Suppose, for example, that in your language you have a t-sound which is made by touching the upper front teeth with the tip of your tongue: this is quite often the case. The difference between this t and the t-sound of English is that the English t is generally made with the tip of the tongue touching the alveolar ridge just behind the teeth. This may not seem much of a difference to you, but a t which is made on the teeth sounds foreign to an English ear, and although it will be recognized as /t/, it will not sound correct in English.

When you study the movements of the speech organs for a certain sound of English, try to compare them with the movements for a similar sound in your language. Try to become conscious of what your speech organs are doing. The exercises which follow will help you to do this.

EXERCISES ON CHAPTER 2

(Answers, where appropriate, on p. 163)

1. Copy Figures 1, 3 and 6. Label all the different parts of the speech organs. Do this several times, until you can do it without looking at the book.

2. Three different actions take place in the larynx. What are they?

3. Which sounds in your language are voiced, and which are voiceless? Which of these sounds are similar except for a difference of voicing, like s and z in English?

4. Can you sing a voiceless sound? And if not, why not?

5. How does the soft palate affect the direction of the air stream?

6. What sounds in your language are made with the soft palate lowered?

7. Make a p-sound and hold it with the lips closed; then, still keeping the lips closed, let the air burst out through the nose. Do the same with t and k. Do the same with b, d, and g and let *voiced* air burst out through the nose.

8. Say several k-sounds quickly one after the other, k-k-k-k, and feel the back of the tongue touching and leaving the soft palate. Do the same with t—first with the tongue touching the alveolar ridge; then with the tongue-tip touching the upper front teeth. Can you do the same thing with the tongue-tip touching the centre of the hard palate?

9. Make the vowels iː, i, e, æ and feel how the front of the tongue is lowered each time and the jaw opens gradu-

ally. Do the same with uː, u, ɔː, ɔ, ɑː and feel how the back of the tongue is lowered.

10. What does the tongue do in making the sounds ai, ɔi, au?

11. Make the flat and curved shapes of the tongue shown in Figures 10 and 11. Use your mirror.

12. Make a t-sound and hold it with the tongue-tip in contact with the alveolar ridge. Now gently bring the teeth together. What happens to the sides of the tongue and why?

13. Put your mouth in an l position and draw breath in and out. Feel it on the sides of the tongue. Do the same with s and feel it on the centre of the tongue. Alternate the s and l positions and feel the sides of the tongue rise and lower as you go from one to the other.

3

THE CONSONANTS OF ENGLISH

There are two good reasons for beginning with consonants rather than vowels. First, consonants contribute more to making English understood than vowels do. Second, consonants are generally made by a definite interference of the vocal organs with the air stream, and so are easier to describe and understand.

The sentence 'C--ld y-- p-ss m- - p--c- -f str-ng, pl--s-' is easy for an English reader to understand even though all of the vowel *letters* have been left out. Similarly, if in actually speaking we could leave out all the vowel *sounds* and pronounce only the consonants most English would still be fairly easy to understand. But look at the same sentence with all the consonant letters left out: '-ou-- -ou -a--- -e a -ie-e o- ---i--, --ea-e.' It is impossible to make any sense out of it, and the same would be true in speaking, because the consonants form the bones, the skeleton of English words and give them their basic shape.

Native speakers of English from different parts of the world have different accents, but the differences of accent are mainly the result of differences in the sound of the *vowels*; the consonants are pronounced in very much the same way wherever English is spoken. So if the vowels you use are imperfect it will not prevent you from being understood, but if the consonants are imperfect there will be a great risk of misunderstanding.

In dealing with the consonants you must first learn how each one is mainly distinguished from the others, the features which it *must* have so that it will not be mistaken for any other consonant. Then later you will learn about any special sounds of that phoneme which need small changes in their formation in different circumstances, changes which are not essential if you simply want to be understood, but which will make your English sound better.

FRICTION CONSONANTS

There are nine consonant phonemes whose main sounds all have friction as their most important feature. They are /f, v, θ, ð, s, z, ʃ, ʒ, h/. For all of them the lungs push air through a narrow opening where it causes friction of various kinds.

f and v

For both f and v the speech organs are in the position shown in Figure 12.

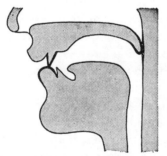

Fig. 12. f and v.

Notice. 1. The soft palate is raised so that no air goes through the nose and it is all forced through the mouth.

2. The bottom lip is very close to the upper front teeth: this forms the narrowing and when air is pushed through this narrowing it causes slight friction.

3. The tongue is not directly concerned in making these sounds, but it does not lie idle; it takes up the position necessary for the *following* sound, so in fiː it will be in the

iː position whilst f is being pronounced, and in friː it will be in the r position, and so on.

The difference between f and v is mainly one of *strength*: f is a strong consonant, v is a weak one. Also f is never voiced, but v may be. And f is rather *longer* than v.

So f is a strong, voiceless, long consonant, v is a weak, perhaps voiced, short consonant.

Put your lower lip and upper teeth close together and blow breath between them quite strongly: continue the sound and listen to the friction—it is not very noisy but can be heard quite easily. Now blow the breath through very gently; the friction is much less and must *always* be much less for v than for f. Alternate this strong and weak friction for f and v; don't worry about voicing, it is not important.

Now say the word *fast* faːst with strong friction for the f. Now say *vast* vaːst with very short weak friction for the v. Alternate these: faːst, vaːst, and be sure that there is very little, very weak friction for the v, but also be sure that it is the lip and the teeth which are causing the friction, *not* the two lips. Keep the upper lip out of the way altogether.

If your language has both /f/ and /v/, the sounds that you use will probably do quite well in English, provided that you are quite sure that both of them have this lip-teeth action, especially the v. Although there is very little friction for v there must always be some; it must not be completely frictionless. Now practice the following lists of words, with long, strong friction for f and short, weak friction for v.

faːst	fast	vaːst	vast	fjuː	few	vjuː	view
fiːl	feel	viːl	veal	fiə	fear	viə	veer
foul	foal	voul	vole	fail	file	vail	vile
feri	ferry	veri	very	fæt	fat	væt	vat
fæn	fan	væn	van	feil	fail	veil	veil

Now try these sounds between vowels. In this position the v will be voiced in English, but the important thing for you is to make it short and weak: if you do this the voicing can take care of itself. (If your language has voiced v anyway, this is fine.) Take special care in this position that the v has some friction, though not too much, and that the friction is caused by lip-teeth action and not by the two lips. Use your mirror to make sure that the upper lip is well clear of the lower one.

sʌfə	suffer	kʌvə	cover
defə	deafer	nevə	never
snifiŋ	sniffing	giviŋ	giving
pruːfiŋ	proofing	pruːviŋ	proving
rʌfə	rougher	lʌvə	lover
soufə	sofa	ouvə	over
seifə	safer	seivə	savour
ɔfə	offer	hɔvə	hover
difaid	defied	divaid	divide
rifjuːz	refuse	rivjuːz	reviews

In phrases we do exactly the same, long strong friction for f and short weak friction for v. Try these:

veri faːst	very fast	veri vaːst	very vast
ai fiːl fain	I feel fine	ai fiːl vail	I feel vile
fain fəːz	fine furs	fain vəːs	fine verse
fɔː fænz	four fans	fɔː vænz	four vans
ə gud fjuː	a good few	ə gud vjuː	a good view

When f and v occur at the end of words, after a vowel, they have an effect on the *length* of the vowel. The strong consonant f makes the vowel shorter, the weak consonant v makes the vowel longer. This is an important general rule which applies to many other pairs of consonants as well: *strong consonants at the end of words shorten the preceding vowel, weak consonants lengthen it.* In the words *safe* seif and *save* seiv, the f and the v have the same features as before: f is stronger and longer, v is weaker and shorter, very short indeed in this position, but the vowels are of very different lengths; in seif the ei is quite short and in seiv it is really long.

Say these words, seif and seiv, and be particularly careful to lengthen out the vowel in seiv, drawl it, drag it out, and then add a very short weak v friction at the very end. Don't shorten the ei in seif *too* much, but do be sure that the ei in seiv is very much longer. Now do the same with the following words:

liːf	leaf	liːv	leave	laif	life	laiv	live
hɑːf	half	hɑːv	halve	straif	strife	straiv	strive
kɑːf	calf	kɑːv	carve	reif	Ralph	reiv	rave
pruːf	proof	pruːv	prove	weif	waif	weiv	wave
səːf	surf	səːv	serve	seif	safe	seiv	save

These words all contain vowel phonemes which are naturally long, that is to say longer than the vowels /i e æ ɔ u ʌ/ in similar positions. The short vowels behave like the long ones when followed by f or v, that is, they are shortest when followed by strong f and rather longer when followed by weak v, although they are never so long as the long vowels when these are followed by the weak consonant.

Try this with the words below: before f make the vowel quite short, and before v make it a little longer, about as long as the long vowels before f. And still make f longer and stronger, and v very short and weak in friction.

stif	stiff	siv	sieve	ɔf	off	ɔv	of
klif	cliff	liv	live	rʌf	rough	dʌv	dove
snif	sniff	giv	give	blʌf	bluff	lʌv	love
ræf	R.A.F.	hæv	have	flʌf	fluff	glʌv	glove

FRICTION CONSONANTS

Now look at the phrases below, and decide which of the vowels have to be longer and which shorter. Remember that there are *three* lengths: (1) short vowels (/i e æ ɔ u ʌ/) before the strong consonant, e.g. stif, (2) short vowels before the weak consonant, *and* long vowels before the strong consonant, e.g. glʌv and weif, (3) long vowels before the weak consonant, e.g. seiv. Now say them with good vowel length and good difference between f and v.

ə hɑːf snif	a half sniff	ə breiv blʌf	a brave bluff
ə stif glʌv	a stiff glove	ə laiv dʌv	a live dove
ə briːf lʌv	a brief love	ɔ seif muːv	a safe move
ə rʌf greiv	a rough grave	ə greiv griːf	a grave grief
ə dwɔːf stouv	a dwarf stove	ə klif draiv	a cliff drive

Some of the most common English words which contain /f/ are: *family, far, fat, father, feel, few, fried, first, foe, four, five, from, friend, front, before, after, afraid, different, difficult, left, office, perfect, prefer, suffer, awful, often, half, off, knife, life, laugh, self, wife, safe, cough, rough, stiff.*

Some of the most common English words which contain /v/ are: *very, valve, visit, voice, value, violent, vast, van, view, ever, never, over, river, seven, several, travel, even, every, heavy, live, of, give, love, move, prove, receive, believe, save, serve, twelve, wave, five, have.*

Sometimes when you are listening to English, listen especially for these words (and others containing /f/ and /v/) and try to fix the sounds in your mind.

θ and ð

θ and ð are also friction sounds, θ is *strong* and ð is *weak*. Both have the position of the speech organs shown in Figure 13.

Notice. 1. The soft palate is raised so that all the breath is forced to go through the mouth.

2. The tip of the tongue is close to the upper front teeth: this is the narrowing where the friction is made.

3. The noise made by the friction for θ and ð is not very great, much less than for s and z.

Put the tip of your tongue close to the cutting-edge of your upper front teeth. In a mirror you will be able to see the tip. Blow air through this position so that you get some friction, but not too much, not so much as for s. Continue the sound and listen to it. θ should make the same amount

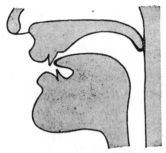

Fig. 13. θ and ð.

of noise as f, not more. Try f and θ alternately until you get the friction right for θ. Now make less friction for ð by pushing the air more gently. The friction for ð when it is properly made can only just be heard. Now alternate the stronger θ and the weaker ð—not too much friction in θ and even less in ð.

All that I said about strong and weak consonants on p. 34 is true for θ and ð. θ is stronger and longer and always voiceless, ð is weaker and shorter and may be voiced. Confusing θ and ð will scarcely ever lead to misunderstanding because they rarely occur in words which are otherwise similar, but if you do not make the difference properly it will be noticeable.

Try the words given below, and be sure (1) that the air passes between the tongue tip and the teeth, and (2) that the friction is never too strong.

θin	thin	ðen	then	θæŋk	thank	ðæt	that
θiŋk	think	ðis	this	θɔ:t	thought	ðouz	those
θi:f	thief	ði:z	these				

Some people may confuse θ with f and ð with v; this is not very important for understanding, since some English speakers do the same, but you should try not to make these confusions because they will be noticeable. Say these words, and be sure that for f and v you are using a lip-teeth action, and for θ and ð a tongue-teeth action.

fin	fin	θin	thin	fɔ:t	fought	θɔ:t	thought
fri:	free	θri:	three	fril	frill	θril	thrill
fə:st	first	θə:st	thirst	fɔ:ti	forty	θə:ti	thirty
ðæt	that	væt	vat	ðen	then	vent	vent
ðei	they	vein	vain	ðɛə	there	viə	veer
ði:z	these	vi:l	veal	ðou	though	voul	vole

Between vowels ð is voiced, but the important thing for you is to make it very short and weak, and let the voicing take care of itself. θ is always voiceless. Say these words:

ɔ:θə	author	ʌðə	other	mɑ:θə	Martha	mʌðə	mother
ɑ:θə	Arthur	rɑ:ðə	rather	nʌθiŋ	nothing	brʌðə	brother
ə:θi	earthy	wə:ði	worthy	bə:θə	Bertha	fə:ðə	further

Now try to keep /f, v, θ, ð/ separate in this position.

ɔ:θə	author	ɔfə	offer	ɑ:θə	Arthur	tʌfə	tougher
nʌθiŋ	nothing	pʌfiŋ	puffing	tu:θi	toothy	ru:fiŋ	roofing
brʌðə	brother	lʌvə	lover	leðə	leather	nevə	never
fɑ:ðə	father	kɑ:və	carver	hi:ðən	heathen	i:vən	even

At the end of words θ and ð affect a preceding vowel in

39

the same way as f and v. Try with some long vowels, and make the vowel specially long before ð.

grouθ	growth	louð	loathe
tu:θ	tooth	smu:ð	smooth
bouθ	both	klouð	clothe
ri:θ	wreath	bri:ð	breathe
feiθ	faith	beið	bathe
mauθ	mouth (n.)	mauð	mouth (vb.)

The only word in which ð occurs finally after a short vowel is wið *with*, but try keeping the vowel at its shortest in the following:

mɔθ	moth	miθ	myth	breθ	breath
deθ	death	rɔθ	wrath		

Some of the most common English words which contain /θ/ are: *thank, thick, thin, thing, thirsty, thousand, three, through, throw, Thursday, thought, thirty, healthy, wealthy, something, anything, both, bath, breath, cloth, earth, fourth,* etc., *faith, health, month, mouth, north, south, path, worth, death.*

Some of the most common English words which contain /ð/ (and some of these are amongst the commonest in the language) are: *the, this, that, these, those, there, their, then, they, them, though, than, other, mother, father, brother, either, neither, further, clothes, leather, together, weather, whether, breathe, with, smooth.*

Sometimes when you listen to English listen specially for these words (and others containing /θ/ and /ð/) and try to fix the sounds in your mind.

On p. 44 you will find more about /θ/ and /ð/ when they are close to /s/ and /z/.

s and z

s is a strong friction sound and z is a weak one. The position of the speech organs for these sounds is shown in Figure 14.

Notice. 1. The soft palate is raised so that all the breath is forced to go through the mouth.

2. The tip and blade of the tongue are very close to the alveolar ridge. There is a very considerable narrowing at this point, *not* near the teeth and *not* near the hard palate.

3. The teeth are very close together.

4. The friction for these sounds, especially for s, is much greater than for f, v, θ and ð.

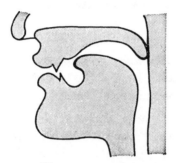

Fig. 14. s and z.

There will be a sound similar to s in your language: make this sound, then keep your mouth in that position and draw air inwards; make small changes in the position of the tip and blade of the tongue until you can feel that the cold air is hitting the tongue at the very centre of the alveolar ridge, not further forward and not further back. z is the weak sound, so when you are satisfied with the strong friction for s, push air through more slowly so that the friction is weaker. Alternate strong and weak friction.

Once again, as for the other consonants, the strong one, s, is longer and always voiceless, the weak one, z, is quite short and may be voiced, but again the *gentleness* of z is the thing to concentrate on.

z is not a common sound at the beginning of words, so confusing s and z in initial position will not generally lead to misunderstanding; but English speakers do distinguish them, so you should try to do so too. Try the following words:

siŋk	sink	ziŋk	zinc	suː	Sue	zuː	zoo
sed	said	zed	Zed	siːl	seal	ziːl	zeal
sɔːn	sawn	zoun	zone	sist	cyst	zest	zest

Between vowels z is voiced, and if you voice this sound naturally in that position that is good; if not, the sound should be made very gently and very short. s is always voiceless. Try these words:

luːsə	looser	luːzə	loser	kɔːsə	coarser	kɔːzə	causer
leisi	lacy	leizi	lazy	fʌsi	fussy	fʌzi	fuzzy
bʌsiz	buses	bʌziz	buzzes	reisiŋ	racing	reiziŋ	raising

At the end of words, after a vowel, s makes the vowel rather shorter and z makes it longer, as with /f, v, θ, ð/, and in this position z is particularly short and gentle—just the faintest touch of a z is sufficient, but the vowel must be good and long. Try the words below and make both the difference of vowel length and of consonant strength:

pleis	place	pleiz	plays	niːs	niece	niːz	knees
kɔːs	coarse	kɔːz	cause	prais	price	praiz	prize
luːs	loose	luːz	lose	həːs	hearse	həːz	hers

And now some more with short vowels:

bʌs	bus	bʌz	buzz	his	hiss	hiz	his
æs	ass	æz	as				

For the speakers of many languages (e.g. French, German, Italian, Arabic, Chinese, Japanese, Russian, etc. etc.)

there are not separate phonemes /θ/ and /s/ but only one which is usually more like the English s. So there is a danger that s will be used instead of θ. The difference between them is that s is made with the tip and blade of the tongue close to the centre of the alveolar ridge and makes a strong friction, whereas θ is made with the tongue tip near the upper teeth and makes much less friction.

Distinguish carefully between all these pairs:

sin	sin	θin	thin	sɔːt	sort	θɔːt	thought
siŋ	sing	θiŋ	thing	sʌm	sum	θʌm	thumb
siŋk	sink	θiŋk	think	sai	sigh	θai	thigh

Now do them again, and be absolutely certain that you do not replace s by θ: there is always a danger of replacing the more familiar with the less familiar sound, as well as the reverse.

Now try them at the end of words (the vowel length is the same all the time because both are strong consonants and shorten the vowel), but s must still make much more noise than θ.

maus	mouse	mauθ	mouth	feis	face	feiθ	faith
mɔs	moss	mɔθ	moth	paːs	pass	paːθ	path
fɔːs	force	fɔːθ	fourth	wəːs	worse	wəːθ	worth

Repeat this exercise and be sure again that you are not replacing s by θ.

The same difficulty applies to z and ð. Both are weak sounds but z makes more noise than ð. Try these words:

zuː	zoo	ðou	though
briːz	breeze	briːð	breathe
raiz	rise	raið	writhe
tiːziŋ	teasing	tiːðiŋ	teething
riːzən	reason	hiːðən	heathen

43

CONSONANTS

zed	Zed	ðen	then
klouz	close	klouð	clothe
leiz	lays	leið	lathe
klouziŋ	closing	klouðiŋ	clothing
maizə	miser	naiðə	neither

Go through these words again and be sure that you are not replacing ð by z *or* z by ð.

Those people who speak languages where /θ/ and /s/ are not separate phonemes usually have a special difficulty when /s/ and /θ/ occur close together in words like θiŋks *thinks*. Because s and θ are both made with the tongue-tip and because the teeth and the alveolar ridge are rather close together there is a danger of using s in both places, or even θ in both places, giving siŋks or θiŋkθ. This must be avoided if possible. /z/ and /ð/ give exactly the same difficulty. Try the following words and be careful to make s and z noisy and θ and ð less noisy: sauθ *south*, ðis *this*, ði:z *these*, ðouz *those*, θaiz *thighs*, smu:ð *smooth*, θiŋz *things*, sevənθ *seventh*, θə:sti *thirsty*, mʌðəz *mothers*, sʌðən *southern*, ðɛəz *theirs*, θisl̩ *thistle*.

Making /s, z/ and /θ, ð/ sufficiently different from each other is even more difficult when they are next to each other in a word or phrase like bɑ:ðz *baths* or bouθ saidz *both sides*. This happens very often in English because /s/ and /z/ are very common at the end of words and /ð/ begins some very common words such as *the, this, that, them*, etc.

Start with a long θ-sound, not too much noise, then slide the tip of the tongue gently backwards to the alveolar ridge, which will give the noisy s-sound. Do this several times, and be sure that you start with a good θ; then gradually make the θ shorter before you slide the tip back to the s position. Now practise these words and be careful to make a distinct difference each time:

mɔθ	moth	mɔs	moss	mɔθs	moths
miθ	myth	mis	miss	miθs	myths
fɔːθ	fourth	fɔːs	force	fɔːθs	fourths

Now do the same with ð and z; start with a long quiet ð and gently slide the tongue back to give the noisier z. Gradually shorten the sounds (but be careful to make *both*, not ð or z alone) and then practise making a difference between these words:

briːð	breathe	briːz	breeze	briːðz	breathes
raið	writhe	raiz	rise	raiðz	writhes
klouð	clothe	klouz	close	klouðz	clothes

Now try going from s to θ; this time gently slide the tongue forward towards the teeth until the noisy s is replaced by the quiet θ. Do this several times and be sure that *both* sounds are heard. Then practise these phrases:

ə nais θiŋ	a nice thing	its θik	it's thick
dʒæks θin	Jack's thin	lets θiŋk	let's think
jes θæŋks	yes, thanks	pɑːs θruː	pass through

Do the same with z and ð and then practise these phrases:

huːz ðis	who's this?	juːz ðæt	use that
əz ðou	as though	dʒɔnz ðɛə	John's there
luːz ðəm	lose them	wɛəz ðə tiː	where's the tea?

And finally some more phrases in which /s, z, θ, ð/ come together in various orders. Always be careful to make one noisy sound (s, z) and one quiet one (θ, ð):

wɔts ðæt	what's that?	bouθ saidz	both sides
its ðɛəz	it's theirs	waiz θɔːts	wise thoughts
hiːz θəːti	he's thirty	wið seifti	with safety
briːð sɔftli	breathe softly	ðiːz θriː	these three

There are various tongue-twisters—sentences which are difficult to say—based on the mixing of these four sounds; for example siks θin θis| stiks *six thin thistle sticks* and ðə liːθ pəliːs dismisəθ ʌs *the Leith police dismisseth us*, but native English speakers find these difficult to say, so there is no need to try to master them. It is much better to concentrate on words and phrases like those above which occur very often in normal conversation.

Some of the very many common words containing /s/ are: *same, sing, sit, Saturday, Sunday, save, see, say, second, seem, self, send, six, seven, side, since, sleep, slow, small, so, some, son, sister, soon, start, stay, stop, still, against, almost, beside(s), least, lost, last, listen, message, mister, Mrs, use* (n.), *face, miss, across, advice, case, cats* (etc.), *takes* (etc.), *pass, less, -ness, nice, piece, perhaps, yes.*

Some of the very many common words containing /z/ are: *noisy, busy, reason, easy, lazy, losing, as, his, hers, cause, use* (vb.), *has, is, lose, was, days, dogs* (etc.), *does, moves* (etc.), *noise, please.*

ʃ and ʒ

ʃ is a strong friction sound and ʒ is a weak one. The position of the speech organs for these sounds is shown in Figure 15.

Notice. 1. The soft palate is raised so that all the breath is forced to go through the mouth.

2. There is a narrowing between the tip of the tongue and the *back* of the alveolar ridge.

3. The *front* of the tongue is higher than for s and z.

4. The lips are very slightly rounded.

Start from s: pull the tip of the tongue backwards a little so that the narrowing is at the back of the alveolar ridge (draw the breath inwards to check that you have the tongue in the right place). Keep this position and put the rest of the tongue in position to say the vowel i, *slightly* round the lips, and push the breath through strongly. ʃ is a much noisier sound than f and θ and only a little less noisy than s. For ʒ the friction is weaker, and shorter.

/ʒ/ does not occur at the beginning of English words but /ʃ/ quite frequently does. Try these: ʃiː *she,* ʃou *show,* ʃɔp *shop,* ʃip *ship,* ʃed *shed,* ʃəːt *shirt,* ʃɑːp *sharp,* ʃɔːt *short,* ʃɛə *share,* ʃain *shine,* ʃuə *sure,* ʃʌt *shut,* ʃuː *shoe,* ʃud *should.*

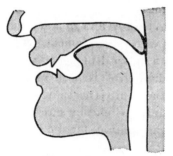

Fig. 15. ʃ and ʒ.

Between vowels ʒ is voiced and if you voice this sound naturally in that position so much the better; if not, make it very gentle and very short. ʃ is always voiceless. There are almost no cases in which /ʃ/ and /ʒ/ distinguish words which are otherwise the same, but practise these mixed words: preʃəs *precious,* treʒə *treasure,* ouʃən *ocean,* iksplouʒən *explosion,* neiʃən *nation,* inveiʒən *invasion,* kəndiʃən *condition,* disiʒən *decision,* preʃə *pressure,* meʒə *measure,* rileiʃən *relation,* əkeiʒən *occasion.*

At the end of words /ʃ/ is quite common but /ʒ/ is very rare and only occurs in a few words borrowed from French: like the other gentle sounds it makes the vowel before it longer, whereas /ʃ/ makes it shorter. Try these /ʃ/ words:

finiʃ finish	rʌbiʃ rubbish	kræʃ crash	krʌʃ crush
wɔʃ wash	puʃ push	liːʃ leash	hɑːʃ harsh

And now these /ʒ/words, making the vowels fully long:

gærɑːʒ garage   beiʒ beige   ruːʒ rouge

As you can see, if you confuse /ʃ/ and /ʒ/, not much damage is done, though since native English speakers distinguish them you should try to too. However, it is much more dangerous to confuse /s/ and /ʃ/ because many words are kept separate only by this difference. In some languages (e.g. Spanish, Greek) there is only one phoneme where English has both /s/ and /ʃ/ and if this is so you must take special care with these phonemes. (The replacement of /s/ by /ʃ/ gives a rather drunken effect to one's speech!) In particular the friction of s is sharper and higher than that of ʃ because the tongue-tip is nearer to the teeth, so practise the pairs of words below and be sure that you move your tongue to the right positions for the two consonants:

sou	so	ʃou	show	sai	sigh	ʃai	shy
sɔk	sock	ʃɔk	shock	siː	see	ʃiː	she
sɔːt	sort	ʃɔːt	short	seim	same	ʃeim	shame
pəːsən	person	pəːʃən	Persian	beisən	basin	neiʃən	nation
lisən	listen	miʃən	mission	misiŋ	missing	wiʃiŋ	wishing
liːs	lease	liːʃ	leash	æs	ass	æʃ	ash
mes	mess	meʃ	mesh				

The danger of confusing words with /z/ and /ʒ/ is very small because few pairs of words have only this difference, but to use one of these where the other is usual will make your English sound wrong, so keep the two separate. Try the following:

rizən	risen	viʒən	vision	reizə	razor	ireiʒə	erasure
reizən	raisin	inveiʒən	invasion	rouzə	Rosa	klouʒə	closure
ruːz	ruse	ruːʒ	rouge	beiz	bays	beiʒ	beige

Some of the commonest words containing /ʃ/ are: *shape, she, ship, sharp, shop, shall, should, short, shut, shout, show, shoulder, shoe, shoot, shine, shore, sure, anxious, ashamed, machine, patient, position, station, motion, nation, ocean, mention, pressure, precious, bush, crash, crush, fish, flesh, foolish, fresh, greenish* (etc.), *punish, push, rush, selfish, wash, wish, dish.*

Some of the commonest words containing /ʒ/ are: *measure, pleasure, usual, division, revision, collision, invasion, vision, inclusion, illusion, provision, explosion, leisure, garage, barrage, rouge, beige.*

h

There are as many h-sounds in English as there are vowels, because h always occurs before a vowel and consists of the sound of breath passing between the open vocal cords and out of the mouth which is already prepared for the following vowel. Before /iː/ the mouth is in position for iː, before /ɑː/ it is ready for ɑː, and so on; so in order to make h-sounds, the mouth is held ready for the vowel and a short gasp of breath is pushed up by the lungs. h does not make very much noise, but it must not be left out when it should be sounded, for two reasons: (1) many words are distinguished by the presence or absence of /h/, like hiə *here* and iə *ear*, (2) English speakers consider that the leaving out of /h/ is the mark of an uncultivated speaker.

Leaving out /h/ is the biggest danger, but a lesser error is to make h-sounds too noisy. Some speakers (for instance, Spaniards, Greeks, Poles) push the breath between the back of the tongue and the soft palate and make a scraping noise at that point. This sounds rather unpleasant to English people and you should avoid it if possible. For the words below, get your mouth ready for the vowel and push a little gasp of breath through your mouth just before the vowel starts:

hɑːt heart	hə: her	hæt hat
hɔːl hall	huː who	hiː he

Say all those words several times and be sure that the
h-sound is there, but not too noisy—just the sound of
breath streaming from the mouth.

Now compare the following pairs, one word with /h/ and
one without:

hɑːm	harm	ɑːm	arm	hiːt	heat	iːt	eat
hedʒ	hedge	edʒ	edge	hɔːl	hall	ɔːl	all
hɛə	hair	ɛə	air	hil	hill	il	ill

/h/ also occurs in the middle of words (although never
at the end of words) and should be made in the same way
as before. If the vocal cords happen to vibrate and give
voice during h this is normal, but there is no need to try
especially to voice the sound. Try these words, with a
definite h, but no scraping:

bihaind	behind	rihəːs	rehearse	riːhauz	re-house
enihau	anyhow	kiːhoul	key-hole	ʌnhouli	unholy
ælkəhɔl	alcohol	bifɔːhænd	beforehand		

h is especially difficult for those who have no such sound
in their own language (for example French, Italian) in
phrases where words with /h/ and words without it are
close together. If you have this trouble you must practise
examples like those below quite *slowly* at first, and be sure
that the words which ought to have /h/ do actually have
it, and, equally important, that those without /h/ do *not*
have it. Try them now, slowly:

hau z ɑːθə	how's Arthur?
aut əv hænd	out of hand
it s ɔːfli hevi	it's awfully heavy
hiz houm z in aiələnd	his home's in Ireland
helən went aut	Helen went out
wiː ɔːl went houm	we all went home

ai hit henri in ði ai	I hit Henry in the eye
ai ɑːskt æn hau ʃiː həːd əbaut it	I asked Ann how she heard about it

Say each of those examples several times slowly with the /h/ in the right places before you speed up to a normal pace.

A few common words sometimes have /h/ and sometimes do not, for example, *he, him, her, have*. This is explained on p. 117.

Some of the commonest words which always contain /h/ are: *half, hand, hat, head, health, hear, here, heart, heavy, hide, high, history, hit, hold, hole, home, hope, horse, hat, house, how, hundred, husband, behind, beforehand, household, anyhow, greenhouse, manhole, inhale, rehearse, coherent.*

STOP CONSONANTS

In stop consonants the breath is completely stopped at some point in the mouth, by the lips or tongue-tip or tongue-back, and then released with a slight explosion. There are four pairs of phonemes containing stops /p, b/, /t, d/, /k, g/ and /tʃ, dʒ/, and like the friction consonants one of each pair is strong and the other weak.

p and b

p is a strong stop consonant and b is a weak one. The position of the organs of speech for these stops is shown in Figure 16.

Notice. 1. The lips are closed firmly and the soft palate is raised so that the breath cannot get out of either the nose or the mouth but is trapped for a short time.

2. When the lips are opened suddenly the breath rushes out with a slight explosion or popping noise.

3. Before the lips are opened, the rest of the mouth takes up the position for the following sound, a vowel

position if a vowel follows, as in *pool*, or a consonant position if a consonant follows, as in *play*.

p is a strong sound, like f and θ and s and ʃ, but it has a special feature which these do not have: it causes the following sound to lose some of the voicing which it would otherwise have. For example, in puːl *pool* the first part of the vowel uː has no voice—it consists of breath flowing through the mouth which is in position for uː. In fact this is what happens for /h/, as we saw on p. 49, so that we may

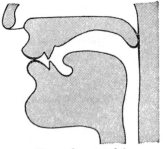

Fig. 16. p and b.

write this voiceless period like this: pʰuːl, where the ʰ represents a voiceless kind of uː. Try making this voiceless uː by itself; it is rather like what you do when you blow out a light. Now put the p in front of it, still with no voice, only strong breath. Now put the vowel uː itself after the breath, pʰuː. Do this several times and be sure that the period of breath is there before the uː starts. Do the same thing with other vowels in the words pʰɔːt, pʰaːt, pʰæt, pʰet, pʰit, pʰiːt. It is very important that the period of breath (which is called *aspiration*) should be there each time. It is this aspiration which mainly separates /p/ from /b/.

Now try /p/ with a following consonant, as in /pleɪ/. Keep the lips closed for p, and behind them put your tongue in position for l; then open the lips and let the breath flow through the l position, with no voice but considerable friction. This gives a voiceless l-sound, which is written ḷ. Do this several times—pḷ, pḷ, pḷ—still with no voice. Now put the ordinary voiced l after pḷ—pḷl—and then go on to the vowel, pḷlei. Do the same thing with the words prei and pjuə, and see that breath flows through the r and j position, giving ṛ and j̊, with friction, before the voiced r and j are heard.

b is a weak stop, and it *never* has aspiration. The vocal cords may vibrate whilst the lips are still closed, but they always vibrate for the following sound, whether vowel or consonant. Try the word buk, and make the b very gentle and without any aspiration. Do the same with bɔːt, baː, bæk, bel, bit, biːn. A following consonant is prepared for whilst the lips are closed and is voiced as soon as they open. Try brait, bluː, bjuːti with a gentle b.

Now try the following pairs of words, and make the p strong and aspirated and the b weak and unaspirated:

piːk	peak	biːk	beak	pit	pit	bit	bit
pæk	pack	bæk	back	paːk	park	baːk	bark
pɔːt	port	bɔːt	bought	pul	pull	bul	bull
praid	pride	braid	bride	pleiz	plays	bleiz	blaze

When p occurs between vowels the aspiration may be less noticeable or even absent, but it will never do any harm to keep the aspiration in this position too. b is of course never aspirated, but in this position it is usually voiced. The most important thing, as with the other weak consonants, is to make it very gentle and short. Try these words:

hæpi	happy	ʃæbi	shabby	sʌpə	supper	rʌbə	rubber
peipə	paper	leibə	labour	ripel	repel	ribel	rebel (vb.)
simpḷ	simple	simbḷ	symbol	əplai	apply	əblaidʒ	oblige

Some learners (e.g. Spaniards) have great difficulty in hearing and making a difference between /b/ and /v/ in this position, so that the words *marble* and *marvel* sound the same. They must take great care to close the lips *very firmly* for b, so that the sound makes an explosion and not a friction. Try these words:

maːb| marble	maːv| marvel	ribən ribbon	rivə river
hæbit habit	hæv it have it	rʌbə rubber	lʌvə lover
leibə labour	feivə favour	beibi baby	neivi navy

In final position (before a pause) p is aspirated and shortens the vowel before it, whilst b is particularly weak and makes only very little noise, but lengthens the vowel before it.

In some languages (e.g. Cantonese, Vietnamese) a final stop is not exploded or is replaced by a glottal stop (a stop consonant in which the breath is blocked by the vocal cords, see p. 19). Speakers of these languages must be very careful to form p and b with the lips, and to open the lips and allow the breath to explode out of the mouth before a pause. Try these words:

rip rip	rib rib	kæp cap	kæb cab
roup rope	roub robe	traip tripe	traib tribe
tæp tap	tæb tab	ræp wrap	græb grab

Those who have difficulty with b and v must again be sure to close the lips firmly for the b and make a very light explosion but no friction. Try:

rib rib	giv give	kæb cab	hæv have
traib tribe	draiv drive	klʌb club	glʌv glove

When /p/ or /b/ are followed immediately by one of the other stop consonants /t, d, k, g/ or by /m/ or /n/ the sound is made a little differently; this is dealt with on p. 87.

Some of the commonest words containing /p/ are: *page, pair, paper, pardon, part, pass, pay, people, perhaps, piece, place, plate, play, please, plenty, poor, possible, post, pound, pretty, price, pull, push, put, appear, April, company, compare, complain, complete, copy, expect, happen, happy, important, open, sleep, cheap, cup, drop, group, heap, help, hope, keep, map, rope, shape, sharp, shop, stop, step, top, up, wrap.*

Some of the commonest words containing /b/ are: *back, bad, bag, bath, be, beautiful, because, become, bed, before, begin, behind, believe, belong, below, besides, best, between, big, black, blue, both, boy, bread, break, breakfast, bring, but, busy, buy, by, brown, able, about, above, September* (etc.), *February, habit, harbour, husband, neighbour, number, obey, possible, probable, public, remember, table, job, rub, rib, rob, club, nib, slab, grab.*

t and d

t is a strong stop consonant and d is a weak one. The position of the organs of speech for these stops is shown in Figure 17.

Notice. 1. The tip of the tongue (*not* the blade) is firmly against the middle of the alveolar ridge, not too near the teeth and not near the hard palate.

2. The soft palate is raised, so the breath cannot escape through either the nose or the mouth, but is trapped for a short time.

3. The sides of the tongue are firmly against the sides of the palate, so that the breath cannot pass over the sides of the tongue.

4. When the tongue-tip is lowered suddenly from the teeth ridge the breath rushes out with a slight explosion or popping noise.

The strong stop t is aspirated in the same way as p and this may be written in a similar way, e.g. tʰuː *too.* Put the tongue tip on the very centre of the alveolar ridge; be sure that only the very point of the tongue is in contact, not the blade; then allow the air to burst out with a voiceless vowel uː; do this several times before adding the normal voiced vowel and be sure that when you do add the uː the voiceless period is still there. Do this several times and each time check the exact position of the tongue-tip and the aspiration. Then do the same thing with other vowels: tʰɔːt, tʰɔp, tʰin, tʰiː, tʰəːn, tʰʌn. Then try the word twin, where the first part of w comes out voiceless and tjuːn where j is also partly voiceless.

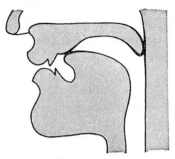

Fig. 17. t and d.

d is short and weak and never aspirated; compare the following words:

tuː	two	duː	do	tɔːn	torn	dɔːn	dawn
ten	ten	den	den	tai	tie	dai	die
tʌn	ton	dʌn	done	taun	town	daun	down
tjuːn	tune	djuːn	dune	twin	twin	dwind‖	dwindle

As with p, when t occurs between vowels, the aspiration may be weaker or even absent, but it will never do any harm to keep the aspiration in this position too. d in this position is usually voiced, but concentrate mainly on making it very gentle and short, and if it is voiced as well so much the better. Try these words:

raitə writer   raidə rider   wetiŋ wetting   wediŋ wedding
lætə latter   lædə ladder   wɔːtə water   wɔːdə warder
waitiʃ whitish   waidiʃ widish   putiŋ putting   pudiŋ pudding

Speakers who find b and v difficult in this position will also find d and ð hard to distinguish. Concentrate on making d with the tip of the tongue firmly against the alveolar ridge, and make sure it is a firm stop rather than a friction sound. Compare:

raidiŋ	riding	raiðiŋ	writhing
briːdiŋ	breeding	briːðiŋ	breathing
loudiŋ	loading	louðiŋ	loathing
lædə	ladder	læðə	lather

In final position t is aspirated and shortens the vowel before it, whilst d is particularly weak and makes only very little noise, but lengthens the vowel before it. However, speakers who tend not to allow t and d to explode in this position should be sure not only to make the difference of vowel length but also to allow the breath to explode out of the mouth. Try these words:

bet	bet	bed	bed	haːt	heart	haːd	hard
leit	late	leid	laid	sait	sight	said	side
set	set	sed	said	brɔːt	brought	brɔːd	broad

d and ð may again be difficult to distinguish in this position. Be sure that d is made with the tongue-tip firmly on the alveolar ridge, and that the breath is released with a tiny explosion. Try the words:

briːd	breed	briːð	breathe	raid	ride	raið	writhe
loud	load	louð	loathe	said	side	saið	scythe

When /t/ and /d/ are followed by any of the other stop consonants, /p, b, k, g/ or by /m/ or /n/ or /l/, the sounds are made a little differently. This is dealt with on p. 87.

Some of the many common words containing /t/ are: *table, take, tell, ten, time, to, today, together, too, top, towards, town, Tuesday, turn, twelve, two, talk, taste, after, better, between, city, dirty, hotel, into, matter, notice, particular, protect, quarter, Saturday, water, writer, about, at, beat, bite, boat, but, coat, eat, eight, fat, flat, gate, get, great, hot, it, let, lot, not, ought, might, put, what.* (Notice also the past tense of verbs ending with a strong consonant, e.g. *missed* mist, *laughed* lɑːft.)

Some of the many common words containing /d/ are: *day, dead, dear, December, decide, depend, different, difficult, do* (etc.), *dinner, dog, door, down, during, already, Monday* (etc.), *holiday, idea, lady, ladder, medicine, body, ready, shoulder, study, today, under, add, afraid, bad, bed, bird, could, would, end, friend, good, had, head, old, read, road, side.* (Notice also the past tense of verbs ending with a vowel, a weak consonant, and /t/, e.g. *owed* oud, *failed* feild, *started* stɑːtid.)

k and g

k is a strong stop consonant and g is a weak one. The position of the organs of speech for these sounds is shown in Figure 18.

Notice. 1. The back of the tongue is in firm contact with the soft palate, and the soft palate is raised, so that the breath is trapped for a short time.

2. When the tongue is lowered suddenly from the soft palate, the breath rushes out of the mouth with a slight explosion or popping noise.

The strong stop k is aspirated in the same way as p and t, and this may be shown in a similar way, e.g. kʰuːl *cool*. Put the tongue in position for k and let the breath burst out in a voiceless uː. Do this several times before adding a normal vowel uː after the voiceless one, and be sure that the voiceless period, the aspiration, comes before the normal vowel each time. Then do the same thing with other vowels in: kʰɔːt, kʰɑːt, kʰæt, kʰil, kʰiːp. Now do the same thing with the following consonants in kliːn, kriːm, kwiːn, kjuː, where the first part of the l, r, w and j comes out voiceless.

The speakers of some languages (e.g. Greek, Persian) may form the stop too far forward in the mouth, with the front of the tongue against the hard palate, before the vowels /e/ and /æ/. This is not a very dangerous mistake,

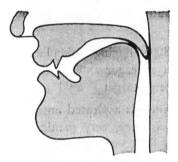

Fig. 18. k and g.

but to English ears the result sounds like /kje/ and /kjæ/ rather than /ke/ and /kæ/, so that it should be avoided if possible. If you have this difficulty, say the words kʌt *cut* and kɑːt *cart* very slowly several times and notice carefully where the tongue touches the soft palate. Then try to keep this position in words such as kept *kept*, kemist *chemist*, kæt *cat* and kæn *can*.

g is short and weak and never aspirated; compare the following words (and do not forget the aspiration of k):

keiv	cave	geiv	gave	kɑːd	card	gɑːd	guard
kəːl	curl	gəːl	girl	kud	could	gud	good
kæp	cap	gæp	gap	koul	coal	goul	goal
klɑːs	class	glɑːs	glass	krou	crow	grou	grow

As with p and t, when k occurs between vowels the aspiration may be weaker or even absent, but it may be kept in this position too. On the other hand g is normally voiced in this position (and of course never aspirated), but concentrate mainly on making it gentle and short. Speakers who confuse /b/ and /d/ with /v/ and /ð/ in this position will also tend to make g a friction sound instead of the correct stop sound. They must be sure to put the tongue into firm contact with the palate and let the breath out with a definite, though slight, explosion. Try these words:

likiŋ	licking	digiŋ	digging	lækiŋ lacking	lægiŋ lagging
wi:kə	weaker	i:gə	eager	θikə thicker	bigə bigger
mɑ:kit	market	tɑ:git	target	æŋk| ankle	æŋg| angle

In final position k is aspirated and shortens the vowel before it, but g is very, very gentle and lengthens the vowel before it. For both consonants there must be a definite explosion, a strong one for k and a weak one for g; a closure without explosion or a simple friction is not correct. Try these words:

pik	pick	pig	pig	dɔk dock	dɔg dog
bæk	back	bæg	bag	lɔk lock	lɔg log
leik	lake	pleig	plague	brouk broke	roug rogue

When /k/ and /g/ are followed by any of the other stop consonants, /p, b, t, d/, or by /m/ or /n/, the sounds are made a little differently. This is dealt with on p. 88.

Some of the commonest words containing /k/ are: *call, can, car, care, carry, case, catch, cause, kind, kitchen, kill, coal, coat, cold, come, cook, corner, count, country, cup, cut, because, become, box, breakfast, excuse, pocket, second, secret, walking* (etc.), *weaker* (etc.), *local, ask, back, black, book, break, dark, drink, lake, like, lock, make, mistake, music, neck, o'clock, quick, take.*

Some of the commonest words containing /g/ are: *game,
garden, gate, get, girl, glass, go, good, grass, great, green, grey,
ground, grow, guess, gun, again, against, ago, agree, angry,
August, exact, forget, language, regular, together, longer, bigger*
(etc.), *tiger, begin, bag, beg, big, dog, fog, leg, rug, plug, flag,
drug.*

tʃ and dʒ

As the phonetic symbols suggest, tʃ and dʒ are stop consonants of a special kind. The air is trapped as for all the
stop consonants, but it is released with definite friction of
the ʃ, ʒ kind. The position of the organs of speech for tʃ and
dʒ is shown in Figure 19.

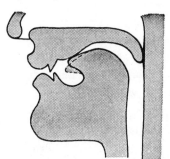

Fig. 19. tʃ and dʒ.

Notice. 1. The tongue-tip touches the back part of the
alveolar ridge, and the soft palate is raised so that the
breath is trapped for a short time.

2. The rest of the tongue is in the ʃ, ʒ position (see
Figure 15).

3. The tongue-tip moves away from the alveolar ridge
a little way (see the dotted lines in Figure 19), and the
whole tongue is then in the ʃ, ʒ position, so that a short
period of this friction is heard. The friction of tʃ and dʒ is
not so long as for ʃ and ʒ alone.

Start with ʃ: say a long ʃ and then raise the tip of the tongue to the nearest part of the alveolar ridge and cut off the friction; then say ʃ again by lowering the tongue-tip. Do this several times. Now start from the closed position, then release the tongue and say ʃ. This is tʃ. (English children imitate a steam engine by a series of tʃ-sounds.) Now try the word tʃiːp *cheap*, and don't make the ʃ friction too long; it is rather shorter than in ʃiːp *sheep*. Like ʃ, tʃ is a strong sound, whereas dʒ is a weak one. Try dʒ by making the friction very weak and shorter than for tʃ. Then try these words:

tʃin chin	dʒin gin	tʃouk choke	dʒouk joke
tʃiə cheer	dʒiə jeer	tʃein chain	dʒein Jane
tʃɔis choice	dʒɔis Joyce	tʃest chest	dʒest jest

Between vowels dʒ is normally voiced, but the important thing is to keep it weak and to keep the friction short: if you also voice it, so much the better. tʃ is still strong and voiceless. Try these words:

ritʃiz	riches	ridʒiz	ridges
kætʃiŋ	catching	kædʒiŋ	cadging
fetʃiŋ	fetching	edʒiŋ	edging
bætʃiz	batches	bædʒiz	badges
wɔtʃiŋ	watching	lɔdʒiŋ	lodging
kitʃən	kitchen	pidʒən	pigeon

In final position tʃ is still strong and voiceless, and it shortens the vowel before it; dʒ is very weak and short, and it lengthens the vowel before it. Try these words:

ritʃ rich	ridʒ ridge	kætʃ catch	kædʒ cadge
səːtʃ search	səːdʒ surge	eitʃ H	eidʒ age
fetʃ fetch	edʒ edge	wɔtʃ watch	lɔdʒ lodge

There may be a danger for some speakers (e.g. Spaniards) of not distinguishing between /tʃ/ and /ʃ/, and between /dʒ/

and /ʒ/. These speakers must be careful to make a definite stop before the friction for tʃ and dʒ, and no stop at all for ʃ and ʒ. Practise with these words:

ʃuː	shoe	tʃuː	chew
wɔʃiŋ	washing	wɔtʃiŋ	watching
wiʃ	wish	witʃ	witch
leʒə	leisure	ledʒə	ledger
ʃɔp	shop	tʃɔp	chop
kæʃiŋ	cashing	kætʃiŋ	catching
kæʃ	cash	kætʃ	catch
meʒə	measure	meidʒə	major

Some of the commonest words containing /tʃ/ are: *chair, chance, change, cheap, chief, child, choice, choose, church, fortune, future, kitchen, nature, picture, question, catch, each, March, much, reach, rich, speech, stretch, such, teach, touch, watch, which.*

Some of the commonest words containing /dʒ/ are: *general, gentleman, January, join, joke, journey, joy, judge, July, jump, June, just, danger, imagine, soldier, subject, age, arrange, bridge, edge, language, large, manage, message, page, strange, village.*

NASAL CONSONANTS

There are three phonemes in English which are represented by nasal consonants, /m, n, ŋ/. In all nasal consonants the soft palate is lowered and at the same time the mouth passage is blocked at some point, so that all the air is pushed out of the nose.

m and n

All languages have consonants which are similar to m and n in English. The position of the speech organs for these sounds is shown in Figures 20 and 21.

Notice. 1. The soft palate is lowered for both m and n.

2. For m the mouth is blocked by closing the two lips, for n by pressing the tip of the tongue against the alveolar ridge, and the sides of the tongue against the sides of the palate.

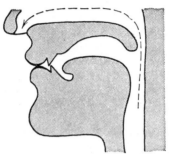

Fig. 20. m.

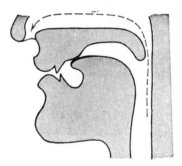

Fig. 21. n.

3. Both sounds are voiced in English, as they are in other languages, and the voiced air passes out through the nose.

Neither of these sounds will cause much difficulty to most speakers. In many languages n is made with the tongue-tip on the teeth themselves rather than on the alveolar ridge, and this should be avoided if possible, but the use of a dental n in English is hardly noticeable. Speakers of some languages (e.g. Portuguese, Yoruba) may have difficulty with these consonants in final position or before other consonants, for example in the words *can* kæn and *camp* kæmp. Instead of making a firm closure with the lips or tongue-tip so that all the breath goes through the nose, they may only lower the soft palate and *not* make a closure, so that some of the breath goes through the nose but the remainder goes through the mouth. When this happens we have a *nasalized vowel*. The word *can* would then be pronounced kæ̃, where æ̃ represents æ pronounced with the soft palate lowered, and *camp* would be kæ̃p. These speakers must be careful to close the lips firmly for m and put the tongue-tip firmly in contact with the alveolar ridge for n and be sure that the closure is completed every time one of these consonants occurs. Practise these words and make m and n rather long if you have this difficulty:

him	him	læm	lamb	ruːm	room	geim	game
limp	limp	læmp	lamp	lʌmp	lump	geimz	games
wʌn	one	tin	tin	suːn	soon	main	mine
send	send	sent	sent	fɔnd	fond	sʌnz	sons

When /m/ or /n/ is found before another consonant, as in some of the examples above, the voiced or voiceless nature of the final consonant has an effect on the length of both the vowel *and* the nasal consonant: this is very similar to the lengthening or shortening of the vowel in examples like *seed/seat*. In the pairs of words below make the m or n quite long in the first word, before the gentle voiced consonant, and make it short in the second word, before the strong, voiceless consonant:

læmz	lambs	læmp	lamp
send	send	sent	sent

CONSONANTS

dʒɔind	joined	dʒɔint	joint
hʌmz	hums	hʌmp	hump
sinz	sins	sins	since
kəmpleind	complained	kəmpleint	complaint

/n/ is often syllabic: that is, it occupies the place at the centre of the syllable which usually is occupied by a vowel. Both the words *lesser* and *lesson* have two syllables: in *lesser* the second syllable is /-sə/, and in *lesson* the second syllable is often /-sn̩/ (n̩ means that n is syllabic) though the word may also be pronounced lesən, with a vowel *between* the /s/ and the /n/. This is true of all the following words, and you may pronounce them with or without the vowel before the /n/. If you leave out the vowel the n will have the same length as the final vowel in lesə. Try these:

pəːsn̩ person   riːzn̩ reason   iːvn̩ even   ɔfn̩ often
fæʃn̩ fashion   əkeiʒn̩ occasion   riːdʒn̩ region   kitʃn̩ kitchen

In words such as *written, garden* a syllabic /n̩/ is almost always used immediately after the /t/ or /d/, that is ritn̩, gɑːdn̩. This requires a special pronunciation of t and d and is dealt with on p. 90.

English people sometimes pronounce a syllabic /m̩/ in words like *blossom, rhythm* blɔsm̩, riðm̩, but more often they are pronounced blɔsəm, riðəm, and that is what you should do.

Some of the commonest words containing /m/ are: *make, man, many, marry, matter, may, me, mean, meat, middle, mind, money, more, mouth, move, much, must, my, almost, among, common, complete, family, promise, remember, simple, summer, tomorrow, woman, am, arm, become, come, farm, form, from, him, home, room, same, seem, some, swim, them, time, warm, welcome.*

Some of the commonest words containing /n/ are: *name, near, nearly, need, neither, never, new, next, nice, night, nine, no, noise, nose, north, notice, now, number, know, knee, and, answer, any, behind, country, dinner, enough, finish, funny, general, journey, manner, many, penny, since, un-, went, winter, again, alone, been, begin, between, can, done, down, green, in, join, learn, on, one, rain, run, skin, son, soon, sun, -teen, ten, than, then.*

ŋ

This is the third English nasal consonant and the only one likely to cause trouble, because many languages do not have a consonant formed like ŋ. The position of the speech organs for ŋ is shown in Figure 22.

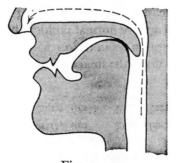

Fig. 22. ŋ.

Notice. 1. The soft palate is lowered and all the air passes out through the nose.

2. The mouth is blocked by the back of the tongue pressed against the soft palate.

3. The sound is voiced.

Remember first of all that the letters *ng* in words like *sing* represent only one sound for most English speakers: a few use two sounds and pronounce the word siŋg, so if you do this it will be perfectly well understood and it is better to pronounce siŋg than to confuse this word with sin. But it is better still to pronounce siŋ as most English speakers do. Your mirror will be useful: ŋ has the same tongue position as g, so start with g and hold this position with the mouth wide open. Notice that the tip of the tongue is low in the mouth and that the back of the tongue is high. Hold this mouth position and at the same time start the humming note that you get with m and n. Be sure that the mouth position does not change, and that the tip of the tongue does not rise at all. Continue the sound for three seconds, watching closely, then stop and start again. Keep your mouth wide open each time so that you can see that the tongue is in the right position. At the end of the sound just let it die away into silence with no suggestion of g. When you can do this easily, do the same thing with the teeth closer together in a more normal position, but be sure that the tip of the tongue stays in its low position. Now try the following words: make the final ŋ long and let it die away into silence:

siŋ sing	sæŋ sang	sɔŋ song	sʌŋ sung
riŋ ring	ræŋ rang	rɔŋ wrong	rʌŋ rung

/ŋ/ does not occur at the beginning of words in English, but it does occur between vowels, where it is more difficult than in final position. The difficulty is to avoid putting in a g after the ŋ, and pronouncing siŋgə instead of siŋə. If you do pronounce siŋgə it does not matter very much because some English speakers also do it; but most do not, so the g should be avoided if possible. Go from the ŋ to the following vowel very smoothly, with no jerk or bang. Try these examples, slowly at first, then more quickly:

siŋə	singer	lɔŋ əgou	long ago
hæŋ ʌp	hang up	rɔŋ əgen	wrong again
siŋiŋ	singing	hæŋiŋ	hanging
briŋ it	bring it	əmʌŋ ʌðəz	among others
lɔŋiŋ	longing	bæŋiŋ	banging

68

The most important thing is to keep /n/ and /ŋ/ separate and not to confuse them. Try the following pairs and be careful to keep the tongue-tip down for ŋ:

sin sin	siŋ sing	sʌn son	sʌŋ sung
ræn ran	ræŋ rang	sinə sinner	siŋə singer
tʌnz tons	tʌŋz tongues		

In some words the sound g is normally pronounced after /ŋ/ before a following vowel, for example in æŋgə *anger*, fiŋgə *finger*. A useful general rule is that if the word is formed from a *verb*, no /g/ is pronounced, as with siŋə, hæŋiŋ, but if not /g/ is pronounced, as in strɔŋgə, formed from the adjective strɔŋ *strong*, and æŋgə *anger*, which is not formed out of a shorter word. Notice the difference between lɔŋgə *longer* formed from the adjective *long*, and lɔŋiŋ *longing* formed from the verb *long*. The sound g is never pronounced before a following consonant, for example: siŋz *sings*, bæŋd *banged*.

If you have the tendency to nasalize the vowel instead of pronouncing ŋ, mentioned on p. 65, you must be very careful to make a firm contact with the back of the tongue and force all the air to go through the nose.

Some of the commonest words containing /ŋ/ are: *anger, anxious, drink, finger, hungry, language, sink, thank, think, among(st), bring, during, evening, hang, -ing, long, morning, ring, sing, song, spring, string, strong, thing, wrong, young.*

LATERAL CONSONANT

One English consonant—l—is formed laterally, that is, instead of the breath passing down the centre of the mouth, it passes round the sides of an obstruction set up in the centre. The position of the organs of speech for l as in /liv/ *live* is shown in Figure 23.

Notice. 1. The soft palate is raised.

2. The tongue-tip (and the sides of the tongue-blade which cannot be seen in the diagram) are in firm contact with the alveolar ridge, obstructing the centre of the mouth.

3. The sides of the remainder of the tongue are not in contact with the sides of the palate, so air can pass between the sides of the tongue and the palate, round the central obstruction formed by the tip and blade of the tongue and so out of the mouth.

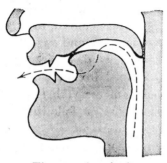

Fig. 23. l as in liv.

4. The sound is voiced and there is no friction (except when it is immediately after /p/ or /k/—see p. 53).

Most languages have a sound like English l, at least before vowels, and this can be used in such words as liːv *leave*, laːst *last*, luk *look*, fɔlou *follow*. Some languages, however (Japanese, for instance), do not have a satisfactory l sound, and such students must be very careful to make a firm contact of the tongue-tip and the sides of the blade with the alveolar ridge. If this is difficult for you try biting the tongue-tip firmly between top and bottom teeth; this will make a central obstruction and the air will be forced to pass over the sides of the tongue. In passing to the vowel the tongue-tip is removed from the alveolar ridge quite suddenly and the sound ends sharply; it may help to put in a very quick d-sound between the l and the following vowel: lᵈiːv *leave*, etc.

Practise the following words, making the l long and the central obstruction very firm to begin with:

liːf leaf	letə letter	lɔst lost	luːs loose
ləːn learn	leit late	laik like	laud loud

When you are satisfied with l in this position try these words, and be sure that the contact of the tongue-tip with the alveolar ridge is complete:

fiːliŋ feeling	felou fellow	fuːliʃ foolish
hɔlədi holiday	biliːv believe	əlau allow

Once you have a satisfactory l before vowels you can use it in *all* positions without fear of being misunderstood; but many English people use different l sounds before vowels and in other positions. For any l the tongue-tip makes the usual firm contact, but before consonants and in final position the remainder of the tongue takes up a shape like that required for the vowel u or ɔː; before vowels the remainder of the tongue is placed as for the vowel i. So the l has a different 'colouring' in the two cases.

Make the tongue-tip contact firmly, and hold it whilst you say i as in sit—the two things must go on *at the same time*, not one after the other; this is the l before vowels and it is known as the *clear* l. Now hold the contact firmly still and at the same time say the vowel u, as in put; this is the l before consonants and in final positions, e.g. in fil *fill* and fild *filled*, and it is called the *dark* l. Many English speakers use only a clear l in all positions, and many others use only a dark l—which is why it is not very important for you to learn both—but most speakers of the kind of English described here do use both kinds of l. The words given for practice above would all contain clear l, because a vowel immediately follows (and this is true whether the vowel is in the same word or not, so both fiːliŋ and fiːl it have clear l).

Whether or not you decide to use the English dark l in the positions mentioned, some of you (e.g. Japanese, Cantonese) will need to be very careful with l before consonants and in final position. The danger, and it is greater here than elsewhere, is that you do not make a firm contact of the tongue-tip with the alveolar ridge, the result being either some sort of vowel sound—fiu, and fiud for *fill* and *filled*, or some sort of r-sound—fir and fird. The sound in English, whether it is dark or clear, must be a lateral, it must have the firm central obstruction and air escaping over the sides of the tongue. In the words below make the l very carefully and be sure that the tongue-tip makes full and firm contact.

ɔːl	all	ful	full	tuːl	tool	sel	sell
bil	bill	fiːl	feel	teil	tail	mail	mile
aul	owl	ɔil	oil	kɔːld	called	pulz	pulls
fuːlz	fools	belt	belt	fiːld	field	kould	cold
mailz	miles						

/l/ is very often syllabic, like /n/ (p. 66), that is, it occurs in a position more usually occupied by a vowel; in words such as *parcel, level, puzzle, lethal, ruffle* most English people would pronounce pɑːsl̩, levl̩, pʌzl̩, liːθl̩ with syllabic /l̩/, but it is also possible to pronounce pɑːsəl, etc., so do whichever is easiest.

After the stop consonants, however, as in *trouble, apple, bottle, middle, eagle*, it is less desirable to have a vowel between the stop and the /l/. Start with *apple* /æpl̩/: as soon as the lips are opened the l is sounded immediately. Do the same with trʌbl̩. For tækl̩, hold the k until the tip of the

72

tongue is firmly in position for l, then release k. Do the same with iːgl. When /l/ follows /t/ and /d/, the stop sounds have a special release, which is dealt with on p. 93. If a vowel creeps in between any of the stop consonants and /l/, you will not be misunderstood, but this is not the usual English habit. Syllabic /l/ is usually dark l, but again the most important thing is to make an l-sound of some sort. Other examples of words containing syllabic /l/ are:

bjutəfl	beautiful	ɔːfl	awful	trævl	travel	wisl	whistle
dæzl	dazzle	tʃænl	channel	kæml	camel	kʌpl	couple
baibl	Bible	tʃʌkl	chuckle	gigl	giggle		

Some students (e.g. Cantonese) may have difficulty in distinguishing between /l/ and /n/ in initial position; this leads to pronouncing laif *life* as naif *knife* or nɔt *not* as lɔt *lot*, and must be avoided. Remember that n is entirely nasal, all the air goes out of the nose; but l is entirely oral, all the air goes out of the mouth. Try this: say a long n, and, whilst you are saying it, nip your nostrils so that the air cannot escape from the nose; this will interrupt the sound. Now say l and do the same thing: if you are making l correctly there will be no change at all; if there *is* a change it means that some air, or perhaps all the air, is passing through the nose, which is wrong for l. Do the same thing with a long s, and notice that nipping the nose makes no difference to the sound; then try l again, until you are sure that you can always make it without any air going through the nose. It will be helpful to think of a slight d-sound in going from the l to the following vowel, as mentioned above—lᵈaif, lᵈɔt, etc. When you are sure that your n is entirely nasal and your l entirely oral, practise distinguishing these pairs:

lou	low	nou	no	liːd	lead	niːd	need
lait	light	nait	night	leibə	labour	neibə	neighbour
let	let	net	net	lip	lip	nip	nip

73

CONSONANTS

Some of the commonest words containing /l/ are: *lady, land, language, last, late, laugh, lead, learn, leave, left, less, let, like, listen, little, live, long, lot, lack, lose, love, low, allow, along, almost, already, always, cold, colour, difficult, early, eleven, else, fault, -ly, help, o'clock, old, self, yellow, able, all, beautiful, fall, feel, fill, full, girl, meal, mile, parcel, people, possible, real, school, shall, still, table, tell, until, well.*

GLIDING CONSONANTS

There are three consonants which consist of a quick, smooth, non-friction glide towards a following vowel sound, the consonants /j, w, r/.

j

This consonant is a quick glide from the position of the vowel iː or i to any other vowel. We usually transcribe the word *yes* as jes, but we might easily transcribe it iːes or ies, on the understanding that the iː or i is very short and that we move smoothly and quickly to the following e. Try the following words in that way, and be sure that there is no friction in the j-glide:

jɑːd yard   jɔt yacht   jɔː your   jet yet   juː you

The same is true in the following words where /j/ is not initial; make a quick, weak iː-sound before the following vowel:

bjuːti beauty   djuː due   fjuː few   vjuː view
væljuː value   njuː new   mjuːzik music

When j follows /p, t, k/ it loses the voice which it usually has, and is made voiceless; this causes some friction to be heard, and it is important to do this because otherwise the stop consonants may be heard as /b, d, g/, and the word *tune* tjuːn confused with *dune* djuːn. Try the following words, making j in the same way as before *except* that you let breath take the place of voice:

tjuːzdi	Tuesday	tjuːn	tune	pjuə	pure
kəmpjuːtə	computer	kjuː	queue	əkjuːz	accuse

Some English people use /tʃ/ instead of /tj/ and /dʒ/ instead of /dj/, pronouncing tʃuːzdi instead of tjuːzdi *Tuesday*, and dʒuː instead of djuː *due*, but this is not generally accepted and should be avoided.

Most American speakers do not use /j/ in words where it would follow /t, d, n, l, s, θ/, pronouncing tuːn *tune*, duː *due*, nuː *new*, æbsəluːt *absolute*, suːt *suit*, and inθuːziæzəm *enthusiasm*. R.P. speakers always use /j/ after /t, d, n/ in such words, but some do not use it after /l, s, θ/. If your model is American, do not pronounce /j/ after these consonants; if not, it is probably better to use /j/ after all of them. /j/ does not occur in final position.

Some of the commonest words containing /j/ are: *yard, year, yellow, yes, yesterday, yet, you, young, your, use, usual, useful, Europe, amuse, beautiful, cure, during, duty, educate, excuse, failure, few, huge, January, knew, music, new, suit, Tuesday, value.*

w

This consonant consists of a quick glide from the vowel uː or u to whatever vowel follows. It is much more difficult than /j/ because many languages do not have an independent /w/. But it is not difficult to learn to say. Start with uː or u and follow this immediately by the vowel ɔː:—this is the word wɔː *war*. The w part must be short and weak, as with j, but the lips must be rounded quite firmly—even English people move their lips noticeably for w!

Try these words in the same way, beginning each with a very short weak uː or u, with the lips well rounded:

wɔtʃ watch	wet wet	wait white	win win	wiː we
weit wait	wɛə where	wud wood	wul wool	

When /w/ follows a consonant it is made in the same way; but the lips are rounded ready for w before the previous consonant is finished. So in swiːt *sweet* the lips gradually become rounded during the s, and when it ends they are firmly rounded ready for w. This is true for all the following words; try them:

swiːt sweet	swim swim	swet sweat
swɛə swear	dweliŋ dwelling	

You must remember too that when /w/ immediately follows /t/ or /k/ the glide is not voiced, though the lips are again rounded during the stop consonant. Try the following words, round the lips early, and blow out breath through them:

twais twice	twenti twenty	twelv twelve	twin twin
kwait quite	kwik quick	kwaiət quiet	kwiːn queen

/w/ is particularly difficult for those (like Germans, Dutch, many Indians) who have a sound like English v but none like w. These speakers tend to replace /w/ by /v/ and say vel instead of wel *well*. This must be avoided and you can do this by concentrating on pairs like those below. For the /v/ words, keep the lips flat and use the upper teeth to make some friction; for the /w/ words there is no friction and the lips are well rounded.

vəːs verse	wəːs worse	vain vine	wain wine
viːl veal	wiːl wheel	vail vile	wail while
vɛəri vary	wɛəri wary	veil veil	weil wail

When you are able to make /w/ easily, be careful not to use it instead of /v/. It is just as bad to say **weri** for *very* as to say **vel** for *well*.

Now try the following similar pairs with the /w/ and the /v/ between vowels, taking care to make a good difference:

riwɔːd reward riviːl reveal əwei away əveil avail
fɔːwəd forward hɔvəd hovered haiwei highway daivə diver

Words such as *which, when, where, why* (but not *who*) are pronounced with simple /w/ in R.P.: witʃ, wen, wɛə, wai, etc. In some other kinds of English (e.g. American, Scottish, Irish) they begin with /hw/. If your model is one of these, you can begin these words with a completely voiceless w instead of the voiced one.

/w/ does not occur in final position.

Some of the commonest words containing /w/ are: *one, wait, walk, want, warm, wash, watch, water, way, we, week, well, wet, what, when, why, will, wish, with, woman, word, work, always, away, between, quarter, question, quick, quite, sweet, swim, twelve, twenty, twice.*

r

This is the third of the gliding consonants, but it does not resemble one of the English vowels as j and w do. The position of the speech organs for r is shown in Figure 24.

Notice. 1. The tongue has a curved shape with the tip pointing towards the hard palate at the back of the alveolar ridge, the front low and the back rather high.

2. The tongue-tip is not close enough to the palate to cause friction.

3. The lips are rather rounded, especially when r is at the beginning of words.

4. The soft palate is raised; and voiced air flows quietly between the tongue-tip and palate with no friction.

Foreign learners often replace this sound by the sound

which is represented by the letter *r* in their own language. Sometimes they use a *rolled* sound in which the tip of the tongue taps very quickly several times against the alveolar ridge (Italian, Arabic, Russian) or the uvula taps against the back of the tongue in a similar way (Dutch, French, German). Sometimes they use a friction sound with the back of the tongue close to the soft palate and uvula (Danish, French, German). Such sounds are perfectly well understood by English people, but of course they sound foreign.

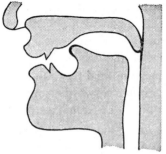

Fig. 24. **r.**

Try approaching the English sound from a **w**. Get the speech organs ready for **w** (remember that this is a short **u** or **u:** sound), and then curl the tip of the tongue back until it is pointing at the hard palate, quite a long way behind the alveolar ridge. Now change smoothly and without friction to the following vowel, as in red *red*. Be careful, if you have an r-sound in your language, not to make it at the same time as the English sound: try to think of English r as a new sound altogether. Try these words and be sure that the tongue-tip is well back in the mouth at the beginning of the glide:

riːd read	red red	rʌn run	rɔː raw
ruːd rude	reis race	raund round	rɛə rare

Between vowels the sound is the same except that the lips are not rounded. Try the following, and concentrate on getting the tongue-tip up and back, then smoothly down and forward again:

| veri | very | mæri | marry | bɔrou | borrow | hʌri | hurry |
| əraiv | arrive | kərekt | correct | əraund | around | ərest | arrest |

In R.P. /r/ only occurs before vowels, never before consonants, so words like *learn, sort, farm* do not contain /r/ (lə:n, sɔ:t, fɑ:m). Other varieties of English pronounce /r/ in these words (e.g. American, Irish, Scottish), so if your model is one of these, you will pronounce /r/ before consonants; if it is R.P. you will not. At the end of words R.P. has /r/ only if the immediately following word begins with a vowel; so the word *never*, if it occurs before a pause or before a word beginning with a consonant (as in *never better*), is pronounced nevə with no /r/ in R.P. But in *never again* where it is immediately followed by a vowel /r/ is pronounced, nevər əgen. This is called the *linking* /r/; some R.P. speakers do not use it (and say nevə əgen), so you may do this if you find it easier, but most people do use it.

Try these phrases, either with or without the /r/:

| betər ɔf | better off | hiər it iz | here it is |
| fɔ:r ɔ: faiv | four or five | puər ould tɔm | poor old Tom |

It is quite usual to hear this linking /r/ following the vowel /ə/ even when there is no letter *r* in the spelling, as in *Africa and Asia* æfrikər ən eiʃə, *Linda and Ann* lindər ən æn. Some English speakers dislike this so-called 'intrusive r', so it is perhaps best for you not to use it. You may also hear it after the vowels /ɑ:/ and /ɔ:/ as in *the Shah of Persia* ðə ʃɑ:r əv pə:ʃə and *I saw a man* ai sɔ:r ə mæn, but here very many English speakers disapprove of it, and you should not use it.

There is danger of confusing /r/ with /l/ (e.g. for Cantonese and Japanese speakers) and also with /n/ (Cantonese). Remember that for n and l there is a very firm contact of the tongue-tip with the alveolar ridge (n being nasal, and l oral, see p. 73), but for r the tongue-tip does not touch the palate at all—it is purely a gliding sound, with no sudden change. Try the following, and concentrate on the very firm contact for l and n, and a smooth glide (like w) for r:

lait light	nait night	rait right
lou low	nou no	rou row
li:d lead	ni:d need	ri:d read
lɔk lock	nɔk knock	rɔk rock

The difficulty is greatest between vowels, so be most careful with the following:

beli belly	beni Bennie	beri berry
kɔ:l əs call us	kɔ:nəz corners	kɔ:rəs chorus
spil it spill it	spin it spin it	spirit spirit
telə teller	tenə tenor	terə terror

After /p, t, k/ there is no voice in r. The tongue position is the same, but pure breath is pushed through the space between the tongue-tip and the hard palate, causing friction. Try with /p/ first; close the lips for p, then put the tongue in position for r, and, as the lips open for p, push breath strongly over the tongue-tip so that you can hear friction before the following vowel:

prei pray	præm pram	praud proud
əpru:v approve	kəmpres compress	dipraiv deprive

Now try /kr/: take up the position for k; then put the tongue-tip in position for r and, when the k is released, push breath through to cause friction:

kri:m cream	kræk crack	kruəl cruel
rikru:t recruit	iŋkri:s increase	dikri:s decrease

When t occurs before r, the tongue-tip for t is placed *behind* the alveolar ridge, on the front of the hard palate, so that when it is removed the tongue is immediately in position for the friction of r. Be sure that in the following words the tongue-tip is a good deal further back than usual for t:

triː	tree	traɪ	try	truː	true	trʌst	trust
ətrækt	attract	ritriːt	retreat	intruːd	intrude		

This /tr/ combination may be confused with /tʃ/; notice that the friction of the voiceless r is *lower* in pitch than that of ʃ. Try the following pairs and be careful to put the tongue-tip in the correct r position for tr:

truː	true	tʃuː	chew	trɪp	trip	tʃɪp	chip
treɪn	train	tʃeɪn	chain	træp	trap	tʃæp	chap

In the combination /dr/ too the tip of the tongue is further back than usual for d and there is friction as the voiced air passes over the tongue-tip for the r. Try these words:

driːm	dream	draɪ	dry	dres	dress	drɒp	drop
drɔː	draw	druːp	droop	ədres	address		

And the following pairs must be distinguished in the same way as /tr/ and /tʃ/:

dreɪn	drain	dʒeɪn	Jane	drɔː	draw	dʒɔː	jaw
druː	drew	dʒuː	Jew	drʌŋk	drunk	dʒʌŋk	junk

Some of the commonest words containing /r/ are: *rain, rather, reach, read, ready, real, red, remember, rest, right, road, roof, room, round, rule, run, write, wrong, agree, already, arrange, borrow, bread, bring, cross, direct, dress, drink, every, foreign, from, great, interest, marry, pretty, price, serious, sorry, story, terrible, true, try, very, worry.*

EXERCISES ON CHAPTER 3

1. Study each section carefully and decide what your difficulties are. Which of these difficulties are *phoneme* difficulties (e.g. confusing /s/ and /θ/ or /t/ and /d/), and which are purely *sound* difficulties (e.g. pronouncing t with the tongue-tip on the teeth instead of on the alveolar ridge)? Which difficulties will you concentrate on?

2. During the time which you give to listening to English, concentrate for a short time on listening to *one* of your difficulties (perhaps the difference between /s/ and /θ/, or the sound of h). When you have really *heard* the sound(s), go back to the lists of words in the different sections and try to make the sound exactly the same as you heard. Use a tape-recorder to help you, if you can.

3. Take any passage of English and mark any one of your difficulties all the way through (e.g. underline every *l* or *r* or both). Then read the passage aloud, and try to say particular sounds perfectly. Don't worry about the others at that moment. Gradually do this for *all* your difficulties.

4. Do a little practice *each day* if you possibly can.

CONSONANT SEQUENCES

In chapter 3 we saw how single consonants are made, and sometimes how a sequence of two consonants should be said (e.g. /pr, kr, tr/ p. 80), but there are many other cases where two or three or four or even more consonants follow one after the other. Some examples are: skiːm *scheme*, kriːm *cream*, skriːm *scream*, neks *necks*, nekst *next*, teksts *texts*.

Some languages (e.g. Russian, German) have many consonant sequences, and speakers of these languages will not have any difficulty in pronouncing most of the English ones. But other languages do not have sequences of consonants at all, or only very few and very short ones (e.g. Mandarin, Cantonese, Vietnamese, Swahili, Yoruba, Tamil), and speakers of these languages (in which two consonants are usually separated by a vowel) may have difficulty in stringing together two, three or four consonants with no vowel between them. This chapter is to help you, if you have this kind of difficulty.

INITIAL SEQUENCES

At the beginning of English words there may be either two or three consonants in sequence.

Sequences of two consonants initially

These are of two main kinds:

1. /s/ followed by one of /p, t, k, f, m, n, l, w, j/, e.g. in *spy, stay, sky, sphere, small, snow, sleep, swear, suit.*

2. One of /p, t, k, b, d, g, f, θ, ʃ, v, m, n/ followed by one of /l, r, w, j/. Not all of these sequences are found (e.g. /pw, dl/ do not occur). The full list is:

/p/ followed by	/l, r, j/	play, pray, pure
/t/	/r, w, j/	try, twice, tune
/k/	/l, r, w, j/	climb, cry, quite, cure
/b/	/l, r, j/	blow, bread, beauty
/d/	/r, w, j/	dress, dwell (rare), duty
/g/	/l, r/	glass, green
/f/	/l, r, j/	fly, from, few
/θ/	/r, w/	throw, thwart (rare)
/ʃ/	/r/	shriek
/v/	/j/	view
/m/	/j/	music
/n/	/j/	new

Start with /sp/: say a long s, then gradually close the lips for p until they stop the s-sound. Keep the s going right up to the moment *after* the lips are closed, and you will not put a vowel between the two consonants. Be careful to start with a long s and do not put a vowel before it. Do this many times until you are sure that there is no vowel sound either before the s or after it. Now add the vowel in words such as:

spai spy   spə: spur   spiə spear   spɛə spare

Do not pronounce əspai or səpai. Start with s and halt it by closing the lips.

/st/ and /sk/ are begun by making a long s and halting it by raising the tongue-tip (for st) or tongue-back (for sk) to cut off the friction. Try:

stei stay   stɑ: star   stɔ: store   stiə steer
skai sky   skɑ: scar   skɔ: score   skɛə scare

Do not say əstei or sətei, etc.

In /sf/ (which is rare) the long s is ended by the lower lip moving up to the upper teeth for f:

sfiə sphere   sferikəl spherical

In /sm/, the s is continued until the lips meet for m, and in /sn, sl/, until the tongue-tip touches the alveolar ridge. (Those of you who have trouble with /l/ and /r/ must be careful not to pronounce sriːp for sliːp *sleep* (see p. 80).)

smail	smile	smouk	smoke	smel	smell	smiə	smear
snou	snow	snɔː	snore	sneik	snake	snæk	snack
slou	slow	slai	sly	slip	slip	slæk	slack

In /sw/ the lips become rounded during the s (be careful not to pronounce /sv/) and in /sj/ the iː, which is the beginning of the j-glide, is reached during the s, so that in both cases the glides start as soon as s ends. Try:

swiːt	sweet	swei	sway	swɔn	swan	swuːp	swoop
sjuːt	suit	sjuː	sue	əsjuːm	assume	pəsjuː	pursue

In the second group of sequences, the second consonant is most often formed whilst the first one is being pronounced. For example, in /pr/ or /pl/ the tongue is placed in the exact position for r or l whilst the lips are still closed for the p, so that as soon as they are open the r or l is heard. In the following examples start with a long first consonant, and during it place the tongue (and for w the lips) in position for the second consonant; then, and only then, release the first consonant:

plei	play	prei	pray	pjuə	pure	trai	try
twais	twice	tjuːn	tune	klaim	climb	krai	cry
kwait	quite	kjuə	cure	blou	blow	bred	bread
bjuːti	beauty	dres	dress	dwel	dwell	djuːti	duty
glɑːs	glass	griːn	green	flai	fly	frɔm	from
fjuː	few	vjuː	view	mjuːzik	music	njuː	new

In /θr/ and /ʃr/ the second consonant cannot be prepared during the first. Be sure first of all that you can pronounce each one separately; say one, then the other, several times.

Then smoothly and continuously make the tongue glide from one to the other so that there is no sudden change between them; try the following, very slowly at first, then gradually quicker:

θrou throw	θriː three	θred thread	θruː threw
ʃriːk shriek	ʃred shred	ʃril shrill	ʃruːd shrewd

Sequences of three consonants initially

These are /spr, str, skr, spj, stj, skj, spl, skw/ and are a combination of the /sp/ type of sequence and the /pr/ type. The s at the beginning is cut off by the following stop, and during the stop the following consonant is fully prepared. Try the following examples very slowly at first; cut off the s by the tongue or lips and, whilst holding this stop, get the third consonant ready, then release the stop straight into the third consonant:

spred spread	streit straight	skruː screw
spjuəriəs spurious	stjuːpid stupid	skjuə skewer
splendid splendid	skwɛə square	

The sequence /spj/ is rare.

Sequences of consonants at the ends of words are more varied than at the beginning mainly because /s/ or /z/ have to be added to most nouns to give their plural forms, as in kæts *cats*, dɔgz *dogs*, fækts *facts*, fiːldz *fields*, etc., and /t/ or /d/ have to be added to most verbs to form their past tense, as in wiʃt *wished*, reizd *raised*, riskt *risked*, plʌndʒd *plunged*, etc. Also /θ/ is used to form nouns like streŋθ *strength* and bredθ *breadth* and numerals like fifθ *fifth* (and all these can have plurals—streŋθs, bredθs, fifθs!).

STOP +STOP

When one stop consonant is immediately followed by another, as in kept *kept* and ækt *act*, the closure of the speech organs for the second consonant is made whilst the closure for the first consonant is still in position. In the sequence /pt/ this is what happens: the lips are closed for p and air is compressed as usual by pressure from the lungs; then, with the lips still closed, the tongue-tip is placed on

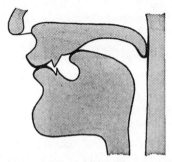

Fig. 25. Double closure in pt.

the alveolar ridge ready for t, so that there are two closures, see Figure 25. Then, and only then, the lips are opened, but there is no explosion of air because the tongue closure prevents the compressed air from bursting out of the mouth; finally, the tongue-tip leaves the alveolar ridge and air explodes out of the mouth. So there is only one explosion for the two stops; the first stop is incomplete.

Figure 26 shows a similar position for the sequence /kt/. First the back of the tongue makes the closure for k, then the tip of the tongue makes the closure for t, then the back of the tongue is lowered without causing an explosion, and finally the tongue-tip is lowered and air explodes out.

Start with kept. First say kep and hold the air back with the lips, don't open them. Now put the tongue-tip in position for t (lips still closed). Now open the lips and be sure that no air comes out, and then lower the tongue-tip and allow the air out. Do this several times and be sure that the lips are firmly closed (we do not say ket) and that the tongue-tip is ready to hold back the breath before you open the lips. Then do the same with ækt, and be sure that although k is properly formed, its ending is, as it were, swallowed, so that there is no explosion until the t is released.

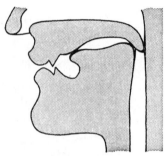

Fig. 26. Double closure in kt.

Now do exactly the same for /bd/ as in rɔbd *robbed* and /gd/ as in drægd *dragged*. Again there is only one explosion, this time a gentle one for the d. If you do make two explosions it will not cause any misunderstanding, but it will sound un-English. What is important is to be sure that the first consonant is properly formed before you take up the position for the second. If you say rɔd instead of rɔbd or dræd instead of drægd, you will be misunderstood.

This 'missing explosion' happens whenever one stop consonant (except /tʃ/ and /dʒ/) is followed immediately by another (including /tʃ/ and /dʒ/), not only at the end of words but also in the middle of words, as in æktə *actor*, or between words, as in red kout *red coat*. Here are some examples for practice:

slept	slept	fækt	fact
rʌbd	rubbed	drʌgd	drugged
tɔp dɔg	top dog	ʃɔp gəːl	shop girl
raip təmaːtou	ripe tomato	eitpəns	eightpence
greit kɛə	great care	hɔt baːθ	hot bath
kwait gud	quite good	θik piːs	thick piece
blækbəːd	blackbird	blæk dɔg	black dog
klʌb tai	club tie	sʌbkɔnʃəs	subconscious
bɔb gudwin	Bob Goodwin	red pəːs	red purse
bæd kould	bad cold	gudbai	goodbye
ai d gou	I'd go	bægpaips	bagpipes
pigteil	pigtail	big bɔi	big boy
lektʃə	lecture	ɔbdʒikt	object (n.)
big dʒouk	big joke	tʃiːp tʃiːz	cheap cheese

When /p/ is followed by /p/, or /t/ by /t/, and so on, there is again only one explosion, but the closure is held for double the usual time. Examples:

slip paːst	slip past	wɔt taim	what time?
luk kɛəfəli	look carefully	bɔb beits	Bob Bates
mæd dɔg	mad dog	big gəːl	big girl

For /tʃ/ and /dʒ/ the friction part of the sound is never missing, so in witʃ tʃɛə *which chair?* and laːdʒ dʒʌg *large jug* the /tʃ/ and /dʒ/ are complete in both places.

When one of the strong/weak pair /p, b/ or /t, d/ or /k, g/ is followed by the other, for example in wɔt dei *what day* or big keik *big cake*, there is only one explosion, but the closure is held for double the usual time and the strength changes during this time. Other examples are:

hip boun hip bone bed taim bed-time blæk gout black goat

If three stop consonants come together, as in strikt pɛərənt *strict parent*, there is still only one explosion, that of the third consonant. What usually happens is that the first consonant is formed and held for longer than usual, the second consonant disappears altogether, and the third is formed and exploded normally. We might write *strict parent* as strik: pɛərənt, where /k:/ represents an unexploded k held for longer than usual. Other examples are:

ai slept bædli	I slept badly
hi: lægd bihaind	he lagged behind
kəlekt peniz	collect pennies
ðei rɔbd kɑ:z	they robbed cars

/pt/ and /kt/ can be followed immediately by /s/ in words like əksepts *accepts* and fækts *facts*. In these sequences p and k are not exploded but the t explodes straight into the s. Be sure to form the first stop firmly. Other examples are:

intərʌpts	interrupts	ədɔpts	adopts
kɔntækts	contacts	prətekts	protects
riækts	reacts		

STOP + NASAL

When /t/ or /d/ are followed by a syllabic /n̩/, as in bʌtn̩ *button* and gɑ:dn̩ *garden*, the explosion of the stop takes place through the nose. This *nasal explosion* happens in this way: the vocal organs form t or d in the usual way, with the soft palate raised to shut off the nasal cavity and the tongue-tip on the alveolar ridge, but instead of taking the tongue-tip away from the alveolar ridge to give the explosion we leave it in the same position and lower the soft palate, so that the breath explodes out of the nose rather than out of the mouth. Figure 27 shows that this is the simplest way of passing from t or d to n, since the tongue position is the same for all three consonants and the only difference is in the raised or lowered position of the soft palate.

Make a t-sound and hold the breath in the mouth, don't let it out; then send all the breath out sharply through the nose (just as in the exercise described on p. 23) whilst still holding the tongue-tip firmly against the alveolar ridge. Do this several times without allowing the tongue-tip to move at all and feel the air bursting out behind the soft palate. Now start the voice vibrating for n as the soft palate lowers and again do this several times without moving the tongue-tip. Now do the same thing for dn, with

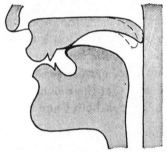

Fig. 27. Nasal explosion in tn.

the voice vibrating through both d and n but the tongue-tip firmly on the alveolar ridge all the time. The effect in both tn and dn is to make the explosion of the stop much less clear than when it takes place out of the mouth; if you do make the explosion by taking the tongue-tip away from the alveolar ridge or if you put the vowel /ə/ between the /t/ or /d/ and the /n/ it will sound rather strange to English ears, but you will not be misunderstood. Try these other similar words:

ritn̩ written britn̩ Britain səːtn̩ certain fraitn̩ frighten
hidn̩ hidden bəːdn̩ burden pɑːdn̩ pardon wudn̩ wooden

Both /tn̩/ and /dn̩/ may be followed by /s/ or /z/ or /t/ or /d/, in words like impɔːtn̩s *importance*, kəːtn̩z *curtains*, impɔːtn̩t

important and fraitn̩d *frightened*. When the third consonant
is t or d the tongue does not move at all—the soft palate
is simply raised again to make the stop complete. For s or z
the tongue-tip is lowered very slightly from the alveolar
ridge to make the necessary friction. Try the following:

pitn̩s	pittance	gɑːdn̩z	gardens	ɔːtn̩t	oughtn't
pɑːdn̩d	pardoned	ridn̩s	riddance	bʌtn̩z	buttons
wudn̩t	wouldn't	ʃɔːtn̩d	shortened		

In words where the n is not syllabic, such as braitnis
brightness and gudnis *goodness*, the explosion is also nasal,
and this is also true when the stop is found at the end of
one word and the /n/ at the beginning of the next, as in
leit nait *late night* and bæd njuːz *bad news*. Try the following
examples, and be sure that the tongue-tip stays firmly on
the alveolar ridge through both t and n:

waitnis	whiteness	witnis	witness
sædnis	sadness	kidni	kidney
ət nait	at night	wɔt nekst	what next?
gud nait	good night	red nouz	red nose
pɑːtnə	partner	laudnis	loudness
stɑːt nau	start now	bred naif	bread knife

Nasal explosion also happens when /m/ follows /t/ or
/d/: the soft palate is lowered whilst the tongue-tip is firmly
on the alveolar ridge and the lips are then quickly closed
for m. It is usually more difficult in this case to keep the
tongue-tip position until after the breath has exploded
through the nose, so you must take care to hold it there.
Try the following:

ʌtmoust	utmost	ætməsfiə	atmosphere
iksaitmənt	excitement	ədmaiə	admire
ədmit	admit	ɔdmənt	oddment

ə bit mɔː	a bit more	wait mais	white mice
eit men	eight men	sæd mjuːzik	sad music
ə gud meni	a good many	brɔːd maindid	broad-minded

When you can do this well, you will not find much difficulty with /p, b, k, g/ followed by /m/ or /n/, in words like heipni *halfpenny* or siknis *sickness*, or in phrases like teik main *take mine* or big mæn *big man*, where the explosion is also nasal. The secret is to hold the stop until the breath has exploded through the nose and only then to change the tongue or lip position for the nasal (if any change is needed). Try the following:

raipnis	ripeness	tɔpmoust	topmost
əknɔlidʒ	acknowledge	frægmənt	fragment
stɔp nau	stop now	help miː	help me
dɑːk nait	dark night	teik main	take mine
klʌb noutis	club notice	big nouz	big nose
big mauθ	big mouth		

/t/ OR /d/ + /l/

t and d are made with the tongue-tip on the alveolar ridge and the sides of the tongue firmly touching the sides of the palate; l is made with the tongue-tip touching the alveolar ridge, but the sides of the tongue away from the sides of the palate so that the breath passes out laterally. The simplest way to go from t or d to l is to leave the tongue-tip on the alveolar ridge and only lower the sides, and that is what we do. It is called *lateral explosion*.

Make the closure for d and hold it; then immediately change to l but be sure that the tongue-tip does not leave the alveolar ridge even for a moment. If you find this difficult try *biting* the tip of your tongue so that it cannot move and then changing to l, until you have got the feeling of the breath exploding over the lowered sides of the tongue; then try it with the tongue-tip in its normal position. Do this several times, and then try the same action for tl. When you are satisfied that the tongue-tip does not move, try the following:

midḷ middle   mʌdḷ muddle   bætḷ battle   litḷ little

The plural ending /z/ and the past tense ending /d/ can be added to /tḷ/ and /dḷ/. For tḷd and dḷd, as in bɔtḷd *bottled* and mʌdḷd *muddled*, the tongue-tip does not move at all; the sides are lowered for ḷ and raised again for d. For tḷz and dḷz, as in bɔtḷz *bottles* and niːdḷz *needles*, the tongue-tip is lowered slightly from the alveolar ridge to give the necessary friction at the same time as the sides are raised to touch the sides of the palate, which they must do for z. Try the following:

hʌdḷd huddled   kəːdḷd curdled   taitḷd titled   mɔtḷd mottled
mɔdḷz models   pedḷz pedals   taitḷz titles   bætḷz battles

In all the examples above /ḷ/ is syllabic (see p. 72), but in words such as sædli *sadly* and θɔːtlis *thoughtless* and in phrases like bæd lait *bad light* and streit lain *straight line*, where the /l/ is not syllabic, the explosion takes place in the same way, with the tongue-tip kept firmly on the alveolar ridge. Try the following:

bædli badly   niːdlis needless   leitli lately
haːtlis heartless   red lait red light   gud lʌk good luck
ət laːst at last   ʃɔːt laif short life

Notice, by the way, that in changing from n to l in words like tʃænḷ *channel* and mænli *manly* and in phrases like griːn liːf *green leaf*, the tongue-tip also stays on the alveolar ridge whilst the sides of the tongue are lowered. Try the following:

pænḷ panel   tʌnḷ tunnel   finlənd Finland
ʌnles unless   təːn left turn left wʌn les one less

Try also the following:

pæn|z	panels	tʌn|z	tunnels
tʃæn|d	channeled	tʌn|d	tunneled

CONSONANT + /s, z, t, d/

Because of the way in which regular plurals are formed in English there are very many sequences of a consonant followed by /s/ or /z/, for example lips *lips*, bəːdz *birds*, sneiks *snakes*, henz *hens*. And because of the way in which regular past tenses are formed there are also very many sequences of a consonant followed by /t/ or /d/, for example, kist *kissed*, lʌvd *loved*, laːft *laughed*, juːzd *used*.

When you make these sequences, be sure always to form the first consonant firmly and then to put the tongue into position for the s or z or the t or d whilst you are still continuing the first consonant. For example, in kʌps *cups* the lips are closed firmly for p and then behind them the tongue-tip is placed in position for s, so that when the lips are opened for the release of p the s is heard immediately. The sounds flow into each other; there must never be an interval or hesitation or vowel between them. Try the following:

kʌps	cups	kæts	cats
wiːks	weeks	laːfs	laughs
dʒɔbz	jobs	gudz	goods
dæmz	dams	təːnz	turns
egz	eggs	draivz	drives
sɔŋz	songs	welz	wells
laːft	laughed	mist	missed
wɔʃt	washed	wɔtʃt	watched
pruːvd	proved	briːðd	breathed
siːmd	seemed	ound	owned
geizd	gazed	dʒʌdʒd	judged
bæŋd	banged	fild	filled

Seven of these sequences /ps, ks, nz, ft, st, nd, ld/ occur in words which are not plurals or past forms; these sequences may then have yet another consonant added to them to form plurals and past forms, for example fikst *fixed* or gests *guests*. For these the tongue-tip must be either raised to make contact with the alveolar ridge to make t or d, or it must be lowered slightly from the alveolar ridge to make the friction of s or z. Be sure that the first two consonants are firmly but smoothly formed before adding the third. Try the following:

læpst lapsed	tækst taxed	brɔnzd bronzed	lifts lifts
rests rests	bendz bends	fiːldz fields	

The sequence /ksts/ occurs in the word teksts *texts*; the last s is again added by lowering the tongue slightly from the t position to give the s friction.

Also, the more common word siksθ *sixth* has θ added to ks. This needs a smooth but definite movement of the tongue-tip from its position close to the alveolar ridge to a position close to the upper teeth; this will not be difficult if you have mastered the exercises on p. 44.

CONSONANT + /θ/

The consonants /t, d, n, l/ are followed by /θ/ in the words eitθ *eighth*, bredθ *breadth*, tenθ *tenth* and helθ *health*. Normally t, d, n and l are made with the tongue-tip on the alveolar ridge, but when followed by θ they are made with the tongue-tip touching the back of the upper teeth. It is then pulled away slightly to give the dental friction of θ.

In the words fifθ *fifth* and leŋθ *length* the tongue-tip is placed in position for θ during the previous consonant, so that again there is no gap between them. There are only a few other words like these—widθ *width*, hʌndrədθ *hundredth*, nainθ *ninth*, θəːtiːnθ *thirteenth*, etc., welθ *wealth*, streŋθ *strength.* Practise these and those given above until you can go smoothly from the first consonant to the θ.

All of these words may then have a plural /s/ added, giving eitθs *eighths*, bredθs *breadths*, etc. The added s should not be difficult if you have mastered the exercises on p. 44. The secret is a smooth but definite movement of the tongue-tip from the dental position of θ to the alveolar position of s. Practise the plurals of all the words given above.

Notice also the word twelfθ *twelfth*, where /fθ/ has /l/ before it. Make sure that the l is properly formed, and then during the l raise the lower lip up to the upper teeth for f and then go on to θ. This word also has the plural form twelfθs. Once again move the tongue-tip smoothly but firmly from the θ to the s position.

/l/ + CONSONANT

Various consonants may follow /l/; we have already dealt with /lz/, /lθ/ and /ld/ on p. 95 and the remainder are not very difficult if you have mastered /l/ by itself. Before any consonant the l will be dark (see p. 71) and the following consonant is formed whilst the l is being pronounced. Try the following:

help help	fɔlt fault	milk milk	ʃelf shelf
els else	welʃ Welsh	ʃelv shelve	bʌldʒ bulge
film film			

Plural and past forms lengthen some of these sequences as before. Try:

helps helps	helpt helped	belts belts	milks milks
milkt milked	ʃelvz shelves	bʌldʒd bulged	filmz films
filmd filmed			

NASAL + CONSONANT

On earlier pages we have dealt with nasal consonants followed by /z/, /d/ and /θ/. Other sequences in which a nasal consonant is followed by another consonant are found in words like sens *sense*, pʌntʃ *punch*, rivendʒ *revenge*, wɔnt *want*, dʒʌmp *jump*, θæŋk *thank*. In all these cases the vocal organs are in exactly or almost exactly the same position for the nasal as for the second consonant; in sens the tongue-tip is lowered slightly at the same time as the soft palate is raised to give the s friction; in all the other cases the tongue and lips remain in the same position in passing from the nasal to the following consonant. Be sure that the nasal consonant is firmly formed and not replaced by nasalizing the previous vowel (see p. 65).

In the word traiəmf *triumph* the m-sound may be formed with the lower teeth against the upper lip, rather than with the two lips, but it is not necessary to do this unless you find it helpful.

There are plural or past forms of all the examples given above, e.g. senst *sensed*, pʌntʃt *punched*, rivendʒd *revenged*, wɔnts *wants*, dʒʌmpt *jumped*, dʒʌmps *jumps*, θæŋkt *thanked*, θæŋks *thanks*, traiəmfs *triumphs*. Remember that with /pt/ and /kt/ the first stop is not exploded (see p. 87). Practise at these examples until you get a smooth change between the consonants.

LONGER CONSONANT SEQUENCES

In phrases one word may end with a consonant sequence and the next word may begin with one, so that longer sequences such as /ŋkskl/ quite commonly occur, for example in ðə bæŋks klouzd *the bank's closed*. As always there is a smooth passage from each consonant to the next, with no gap. If you have mastered the initial and final sequences, the only difficulty will be to pass smoothly from the last consonant of the final sequence to the first of the initial sequence, with no vowel or interval between. This is done, as before, by putting the vocal organs in position for the following consonant during the previous one. The examples below will give you practice in sequences of increasing length.

Three consonants

best mæn	best man	pəhæps nɔt	perhaps not
fiks ðis	fix this	help miː	help me
θæŋk juː	thank you	tʃeinʒ wʌn	change one
wɔtʃ krikit	watch cricket	tɔːl triː	tall tree
nais tjuːn	nice tune	laud krai	loud cry
lɔŋ skəːt	long skirt	peidʒ twenti	page twenty

Four consonants

nekst sʌndi	next Sunday	twelfθ nait	twelfth night
bɔt|d wain	bottled wine	hiː θæŋkt ðəm	he thanked them
vaːst skeil	vast scale		
streindʒ driːm	strange dream	ðæts truː	that's true
smɔːl skwɛə	small square	fifθ flɔː	fifth floor
big splæʃ	big splash	lɔŋ striːt	long street
gud stjuːdn̩t	good student		

Five consonants

milks friː	milk's free	prɔmpt staːt	prompt start
mikst swiːts	mixed sweets	plaːnts ʃriv|	plants shrivel
bent spriŋ	bent spring	ækt stjuːpidli	act stupidly
bent skruː	bent screw	ðæts splendid	that's splendid

Six consonants

nekst spriŋ	next Spring	hindʒd skriːn	hinged screen
hiː θiŋks streit	he thinks straight	ai helpt stjuət	I helped Stuart

a fenst skwɛə   a fenced   twelfθ striːt   Twelfth Street
                square

Seven consonants

ðə teksts stjuːpid   the text's stupid
ʃiː tempts streindʒəz   she tempts strangers

EXERCISES ON CHAPTER 4

1. Does your language have sequences of two, three, four or more consonants? If so, list the ones which are similar to English sequences.

2. Does your language have stop + stop sequences? Practise again the examples on p. 89.

3. Be sure that you can distinguish the following: spy, espy; state, estate; scape, escape; support, sport; succumb, scum; polite, plight; terrain, train; below, blow; strange, estrange; ascribe, scribe; esquire, squire; astute, stewed; ticket, ticked; wrapped, rapid, wrap it.

4. Does your language have nasal explosion (p. 90) or lateral explosion (p. 93)? Practise those examples again.

5. Practise again all the other examples in this chapter, being very careful to follow the instructions given. Finish with the longer sequences on p. 99.

5

THE VOWELS OF ENGLISH

Vowels are made by voiced air passing through different mouth-shapes; the differences in the shape of the mouth are caused by different positions of the tongue and of the lips. It is easy to see and to feel the lip differences, but it is very difficult to see or to feel the tongue differences, and that is why a detailed description of the tongue position for a certain vowel does not really help us to pronounce it well.

Vowels must be learned by *listening and imitating*: I could tell you that the English vowel ɔː as in *saw* is made by rounding the lips and by placing the back of the tongue in a position mid-way between the highest possible and the lowest possible position, but it would be much more helpful if I could simply say the sound for you and get you to imitate me. Since I cannot do this I must leave the listening and imitating to you. So spend some of your listening time on the vowels.

As I said at the beginning of chapter 3 English speakers vary quite a lot in their vowel sounds; the iː-sounds used by an Australian, an American and a Scotsman are all different, but they are all recognized quite easily as /iː/. So the actual sounds that you use for the English vowels are not so important as the differences that you make between them. There must be *differences between* the vowels, and that is what we will concentrate on.

In your language you will have a vowel which is like the English iː in *see*, and one which is like the English ʌ in *sun*, and almost certainly one which is like the English e in *get*. They may not be *exactly* the same as the English vowels you hear in listening to English, but they will do for a starting-point. Say the words biːd *bead* and bed *bed* several times and listen carefully to the sound of the vowels; then try to say a vowel which is *between* the other two, and different from both, not biːd and not bed, but . . .bid—that will be the vowel in bid. You need three different vowels for the three words *bead, bid* and *bed*. Be sure that the middle vowel is *different* and *between* the other two: one thing which will help you to distinguish iː from i is that iː is longer than i as well as different in the quality of the sound. Practise those three words (and listen for them in English) until you are sure that you can keep them separate. The most likely difficulty is that you will confuse /iː/ with /i/, so be sure that i is nearer in quality to e and that it is always shorter than iː.

Remember that when the vowels are followed by a strong consonant they are shorter than when they are followed by a weak consonant, so that *beat, bit* and *bet* all have shorter vowels than *bead, bid* and *bed*, but even so the vowel iː is always longer than the vowels i and e in any one set. Now practise the following sets and pay attention to both the length of the vowels and their quality:

liːd	lead	lid	lid	led	led
wiːt	wheat	wit	wit	wet	wet
biːn	been	bin	bin	ben	Ben
tʃiːk	cheek	tʃik	chick	tʃek	check
fiːl	feel	fil	fill	fel	fell
riːtʃ	reach	ritʃ	rich	retʃ	wretch

Now you need another vowel between /e/ and /ʌ/, that is the vowel /æ/. Say the words bed *bed* and bʌd *bud* several times and be sure that your mouth is quite wide open for the vowel of bʌd. Listen to the vowels carefully and then try to say a vowel which is *between* those two, a vowel which sounds a bit like e and a bit like ʌ but which is different from both. You *must* have different vowels in *bed*, *bad* and *bud*. Practise those three words until you can always make a difference between them; they all have comparatively short vowels so that length differences will not help you here.

Practise the following sets and be sure that each word really sounds different:

ten	ten	tæn	tan	tʌn	ton
bet	bet	bæt	bat	bʌt	but
pen	pen	pæn	pan	pʌn	pun
seks	sex	sæks	sacks	sʌks	sucks
ded	dead	dæd	Dad	dʌd	dud
meʃ	mesh	mæʃ	mash	mʌʃ	mush

Now try all five of these vowels in the sets given below: you will see that there are gaps in some of the sets, where no word exists, for instance there is no word lek; but for practice you can fill in the gaps too. Some of the words are rather uncommon, but don't worry about the meanings— just be sure that the vowel sounds are different:

biːd	bead	bid	bid	bed	bed	bæd	bad	bʌd	bud
liːk	leak	lik	lick			læk	lack	lʌk	luck
hiːl	heel	hil	hill	hel	hell	hæl	Hal	hʌl	hull
tiːn	teen	tin	tin	ten	ten	tæn	tan	tʌn	ton
niːt	neat	nit	knit	net	net	næt	gnat	nʌt	nut
liːst	least	list	list	lest	lest			lʌst	lust
riːm	ream	rim	rim			ræm	ram	rʌm	rum
biːt	beat	bit	bit	bet	bet	bæt	bat	bʌt	but

In England when the doctor wants to look into your mouth and examine your throat he asks you to say *Ah*, that is the vowel ɑː, because for this vowel the tongue is very low and he can see over it to the back of the palate and the pharynx. So if you have no vowel exactly like ɑː in your language you may find a mirror useful—keep your mouth wide open and play with various vowel sounds until you find one which allows you to see the very back of the soft palate quite clearly; this will be similar to an English ɑː, but you must compare it with the ɑː vowels that you hear when you listen to English and adjust your sound if necessary. Remember that /ɑː/ is a long vowel. The short vowel /ɔ/ is a bit like /ɑː/ in quality though of course they must be kept separate. For ɔ the lips may be slightly rounded, for ɑː they are not. Try the following sets:

lʌk	luck	lɑːk	lark	lɔk	lock
kʌd	cud	kɑːd	card	kɔd	cod
dʌk	duck	dɑːk	dark	dɔk	dock
lʌst	lust	lɑːst	last	lɔst	lost
bʌks	bucks	bɑːks	barks	bɔks	box
kʌp	cup	kɑːp	carp	kɔp	cop

In your language there will be a vowel which is similar to the English /uː/ in *two*. The /uː/ in English, like /iː/ and /ɑː/, is always longer than the other vowels. Between /ɔ/ and /uː/ you need to make two other vowels, ɔː, a long one, as in lɔː *law*, and u, a short one, as in put *put*. For ɔː the mouth is less open than for ɔ and the lips are more rounded, but ɔː is nearer in quality to ɔ than to uː. For u the lips are also rounded, but the sound is nearer in quality to uː. All four vowels, /ɔ, ɔː, u, uː/, must be kept separate, and the differences of length will help in this. Try the following sets:

ʃɔd	shod	ʃɔːd	shored	ʃud	should	ʃuːd	shoed
kɔd	cod	kɔːd	cord	kud	could	kuːd	cooed
wɔd	wad	wɔːd	ward	wud	would	wuːd	wooed
lɔk	lock			luk	look	luːk	Luke
pɔl	Poll	pɔːl	Paul	pul	pull	puːl	pool

The vowel /əː/ as in həː *her* is a long vowel which is not very close in quality to any of the other vowels and usually sounds rather vague and indistinct to the foreign learner. You must listen to the vowel especially carefully and try to imitate the indistinctness of it (though to an English listener it sounds quite distinct!). Two things will help: keep your teeth quite close together and do not round your lips at all—smile when you say it! The two commonest mistakes with /əː/ are, first, to replace it by /er/ or by some vowel in your own language which has lip-rounding but which is not likely to be confused with any other English vowel, and second, and more important, it is replaced by /ɑː/ by Japanese speakers and speakers of many African languages and others. In the first case there is no danger of misunderstanding although the vowel will sound strange; in the second case there is danger of misunderstanding, since words like həːt *hurt* and hɑːt *heart* will be confused.

In your listening-time pay special attention to /əː/ and experiment (always with teeth close together and a smile on your face) until you approach the right quality; then make sure that you can distinguish it from /ɑː/—which has the teeth further apart—in the following pairs:

pəːs purse	pɑːs pass	bəːn burn	bɑːn barn
həːd heard	hɑːd hard	fəːm firm	fɑːm farm
pəːtʃt perched	pɑːtʃt parched	ləːks lurks	lɑːks larks

The vowel /ə/ in bənɑːnə *banana* is the commonest of the English vowels and is a short version of /əː/. It is particularly short and indistinct when it is not final, e.g. in əgen *again*, kəntein *contain*, poustmən *postman*. In final position, that is before a pause, as in betə *better*, eiʃə *Asia*, kɔlə *collar*, the vowel sounds more like /ʌ/, though it is not usually so clear.

There are two main difficulties with this vowel: first, to

identify it, that is, to know when it is this vowel you should be aiming at; and second, to get the right quality. In the first case, do not be deceived by English spelling: there is no single letter which always stands for this vowel, so rely on your ear—listen very carefully and you will hear dozens of examples of /ə/ in every bit of English you listen to. In the second case, it is often useful to think of leaving out the vowel altogether in words such as kəndem *condemn*, sætədi *Saturday*, dʒent|mən *gentleman*, where /ə/ comes between consonants. Of course, you will not really leave out the vowel, but you will have a minimum vowel and that is what /ə/ is. Then in initial position, as in ətəmpt *attempt*, əkaunt *account*, əbzəːv *observe*, you must again keep it very short and very obscure. But in final position it need not be so short and it may be more like ʌ, with the mouth a little more open than in other positions.

Try the following examples:

In medial position

pəhæps	perhaps	kəntein	contain
entətein	entertain	imbærəs	embarrass
dinəz	dinners	hindəd	hindered
æmətəː	amateur	glæmərəs	glamorous
kʌmfətəbl̩	comfortable	kəmpounənt	component
ignərənt	ignorant	kærəktəz	characters
ʌndəstænd	understand	menəs	menace
pailət	pilot	terəbl̩	terrible
pəːmənənt	permanent	kəreidʒəs	courageous

In initial position

əbei	obey	ətend	attend
əlau	allow	əbstrʌkt	obstruct
əmaunt	amount	ətʃiːv	achieve
ədɔː	adore	əkaunt	account

VOWELS

ənɔi	annoy	əsaid	aside
əpruːv	approve	əgriː	agree
əpiə	appear	ədʒəːn	adjourn
əfens	offence		

In final position

suːnə	sooner	seilə	sailor
meʒə	measure	kɔlə	collar
sʌlfə	sulphur	ʃoufə	chauffeur
æfrikə	Africa	əmerikə	America
pəːʃə	Persia	kænədə	Canada
flætərə	flatterer	ədmaiərə	admirer
kʌlə	colour	zefə	zephyr
piktʃə	picture	tʃainə	China
məːdərə	murderer	kəmpouzə	composer

More examples of /ə/ will be found in the next chapter when we consider the *weak forms* of certain words, such as *at* and *for* in ət taimz *at times* and fə juː *for you*.

DIPHTHONGS

A diphthong is a glide from one vowel to another, and the whole glide acts like one of the long, simple vowels; so we have biː, baː, bɔː and also bei, bou, bai, bau, bɔi, biə, bɛə, buə. The diphthongs of English are in three groups: those which end in /u/, /ou, au/, those which end in /i/, /ei, ai, ɔi/, and those which end in /ə/, /iə, ɛə, uə/.

ou, au

Both these diphthongs end with u rather than uː although you will not be misunderstood if you do use uː. To get ou as in sou *so*, start with səː and then glide away to u with the lips getting slightly rounded and the sound becoming less loud as the glide progresses. Be sure that the first part of the diphthong is ə: (a real English ə:!) and not ɔ: or any-thing like it, and be sure that the sound *is* a diphthong, not a simple vowel of the ɔ: type. /ou/ and /ɔ:/ must be kept quite separate: try the following:

lou	low	lɔ:	law	sou	so	sɔ:	saw
snou	snow	snɔ:	snore	bout	boat	bɔ:t	bought
klouz	close	klɔ:z	claws	kouk	coke	kɔ:k	cork
koul	coal	kɔ:l	call				

For au start with ʌ. Say tʌn *ton*, and then after the ʌ-sound add an u; this should give taun *town*. /au/ is not difficult for most people. Be sure that /au/ and /ou/ are different. Try the following:

nau	now	nou	know
laud	loud	loud	load
faund	found	found	phoned
rau	row (quarrel)	rou	row (line)
daut	doubt	dout	dote
taunz	towns	tounz	tones

Remember when you practise these examples that diphthongs are shorter before strong consonants and longer before weak ones, just like the other vowels, so bout *boat* has a shorter diphthong than klouz *close* and daut *doubt* a shorter one than laud *loud*. Go back over all those examples and get the lengths right. When no consonant follows, as in lou *low*, the diphthong is at its longest.

ei, ai, ɔi

These diphthongs all end in i, not i: (though it is not serious if you do use i: finally). ei begins with e as in *men*. Say men and then add i after e, gliding smoothly from e to i and making the sound less loud as the glide progresses— this will give mein *main*. The most common mistake is to

use a long, simple vowel, so try to be sure that there is a
glide from e to i; however, if you do use a simple vowel for
/ei/ it will not be misunderstood—some accents of English
(e.g. Scottish) do the same. But /ei/ and /e/ must be quite
separate. Try the following:

leit late	let let	seil sail	sel sell
peipə paper	pepə pepper	treid trade	tred tread
reik rake	rek wreck	feil fail	fel fell

ai glides from ʌ to i, and the loudness becomes less as the
glide progresses. Say fʌn *fun*, and then add i after the ʌ,
with a smooth glide; this will give you fain *fine*. Be sure that
/ai/ is separate from /ei/:

wait white	weit wait	laid lied	leid laid
rais rice	reis race	raiz rise	reiz raise
laik like	leik lake	fail file	feil fail

ɔi glides from ɔː to i, and as usual the loudness becomes
less during the glide. Say dʒɔː *jaw* and then add i, as before.
This will give you dʒɔi *joy*. The ɔː sound is not as long in ɔi
as it is when it is alone, as in dʒɔː. /ɔi/ is not a very common
diphthong and it is not likely to be confused with any other
vowel or diphthong. Try these words:

bɔi boy	tɔi toy	ənɔi annoy	nɔiz noise
ɔil oil	dʒɔin join	əvɔid avoid	bɔilz boils
vɔis voice	hɔist hoist	dʒɔint joint	lɔitə loiter

iə, ɛə, uə

These are all glides to the sort of ə-sound found in final
position, as described on p. 106. iə glides from i (not iː) to
this ə in words like hiə *hear*, niə *near*, etc. If you do use iː
at the beginning of the glide it will sound a bit strange but
you will not be misunderstood. Try the following:

iə	ear	jiə	year	biə	beer	kliə	clear
fiə	fear	riəl	real	biəd	beard	aidiəz	ideas
kəriən	Korean	fiəs	fierce	piəs	pierce	niərə	nearer
riəli	really						

Words such as fʌniə *funnier* and glɔːriəs *glorious*, where /iə/ is the result of adding an ending /ə/ or /əs/ to a word which ends with /i/, should be pronounced in the same way as the iə in *hear*, *near*, etc. The same is true for words such as indiə *India*, ɛəriə *area*, juːniən *union*, etc.

To make ɛə, start with the word hæz *has* (with the proper English æ, between e and ʌ) and then add ʌ after the æ, gliding smoothly from æ to ʌ; this will give you the word hɛəz *hairs*. Notice that the beginning of the diphthong is æ rather than e. You must keep /iə/ and /ɛə/ quite separate; try the following:

hiə	here	hɛə	hair	biə	beer	bɛə	bare
stiəd	steered	stɛəd	stared	iəz	ears	ɛəz	airs
riəli	really	rɛəli	rarely	wiəri	weary	wɛəri	wary

uə starts from u (not uː) and glides to ə; if you use uː at the beginning of the glide it will sound a bit strange but you will not be misunderstood. Try the following:

puə	poor	ʃuə	sure	kjuə	cure
ʃuəli	surely	inʃuərəns	insurance	tuərist	tourist
fjuəriəs	furious	kjuəriɔsəti	curiosity	pjuəli	purely
pjuə	pure				

All these words may also be pronounced with /ɔː/ instead of /uə/ in R.P., pɔː, ʃɔː, kjɔː, etc. Other words, like *fewer*, *bluer*, *continuous*, are also usually pronounced with /uə/— fjuə, bluə, kəntinjuəs—though they can always be pronounced with /uːə/—fjuːə, bluːə, kəntinjuːəs—and in any case they must not be pronounced with /ɔː/. This is also true for *cruel* and *jewel* which must have either /uə/ or /uːə/.

VOWEL SEQUENCES

There are vowel sequences as well as consonant sequences but they are not so difficult. In general, when one vowel (or diphthong) follows another you should pronounce each one quite normally but with a smooth glide between them. The most common sequences are formed by adding /ə/ to a diphthong, especially to /ai/ and /au/ in words like faiə *fire* and auə *our*. When you listen to these two sequences —/aiə, auə/—you will notice that the i in *fire* and the u in *our* are rather weak; in fact both sequences may sound rather like ɑː. It is probably best for you not to imitate this but to pronounce the sequences as ai +ə and au +ə, though the i and the u should not be made too strong. Try the following:

taiə	tyre	tauə	tower
traiəl	trial	trauəl	trowel
kwaiət	quiet	taiəd	tired
kauəd	coward	pauəful	powerful
baiə	buyer	bauə	bower
flaiə	flyer	flauə	flower
aiən	iron	raiət	riot
auəz	ours	ʃauəri	showery

The less common sequences /eiə, ouə, ɔiə/ should be pronounced with the normal diphthong smoothly followed by ə. The i and u need not be weakened at all. Try:

greiə	greyer	pleiə	player	bitreiəl	betrayal
grouə	grower	θrouə	thrower	fɔlouəz	followers
implɔiə	employer	rɔiəl	royal	lɔiəz	lawyers

/iː/ and /uː/ are also followed by /ə/ in words like *freer* and *bluer* which may be pronounced friːə or friə, and bluːə or bluə, as we have seen.

The verb ending -*ing* /iŋ/ gives various sequences in words like the following:

biːiŋ	being	siːiŋ	seeing
duːiŋ	doing	stjuːiŋ	stewing
əlauiŋ	allowing	bauiŋ	bowing
drɔːiŋ	drawing	sɔːiŋ	sawing
gouiŋ	going	nouiŋ	knowing

In words like *saying, enjoying, flying*, where -*ing* follows a word ending with /ei/, /ɔi/ or /ai/, it is common to pronounce seiŋ, indʒɔiŋ, flaiŋ, if you find this easier.

In words like *carrying, pitying*, etc., where a word which ends with /i/ has /iŋ/ added to it, it is usual (and best for you) to pronounce kæriːiŋ, pitiːiŋ, etc., although kæri and piti are the normal forms.

Other vowel sequences are found both within words and between words. These also should be performed with a smooth glide between the vowels. (See also p. 128.) Here are some examples:

keiɔs	chaos	ruin	ruin
biɔnd	beyond	riækt	react
bluːiʃ	bluish	grei aid	grey-eyed
ðiː end	the end	mai oun	my own
	baiɔgrəfi	biography	
	kouɔpəreit	co-operate	
	juː ɑːnt	you aren't	
	gou aut	go out	

tuː auəz two hours mei ai ou it tuː juː may I owe it to you?

EXERCISES ON CHAPTER 5

1. What vowels and diphthongs do you have in your language? Which of the English ones cause you difficulty?

2. During your listening-time listen carefully to one of

the difficult vowels at a time and try to get the sound of it into your head. Make a list of twenty words containing each difficult vowel and practise them.

3. Go back and practise all the examples given in this chapter, and concentrate on making *differences* between the different vowels.

4. Is the length of vowels important in your language? Practise making the difference between the long vowels (including the diphthongs) and the short vowels of English. Don't forget that vowel length is affected by following strong and weak consonants; complete the following list for all the vowels and practise it, thinking about vowel length:

biːd	biːt
hiz	his
sed	set

5. Make a list of phrases like the ones on p. 112, where a vowel or diphthong at the end of one word is immediately followed by another at the beginning of the next. Practise saying them smoothly, with no break between the vowels.

WORDS IN COMPANY

When we talk we do not talk in single words but in groups of words spoken continuously, with no break or pause; we may pause after a group, but not during it. These groups may be long, for example, *However did you manage to do it so neatly and tidily?*, or they may be short, as when we say simply *Yes* or *No*, or they may be of intermediate length, like *How did you do it?* or *Come over here a minute*. When we have longer things to say we break them up into manageable groups like this: ‖*Last Wednesday* | *I wanted to get up to London early* ‖ *so I caught a train* | *about half an hour before my usual one* ‖ *and I got to work* | *about half past eight*‖.

When one group is very closely connected grammatically to the next, there is a very slight pause, marked by (|). When two groups are not so closely connected, there is a longer pause, marked by (‖), and this double bar is also used to mark the end of a complete utterance. It is not usually difficult to see how a long utterance can be broken up into shorter groups, but when you listen to English notice how the speakers do it both in reading and in conversation.

In the group *I could hardly believe my eyes* the words *hardly*, *believe* and *eyes* are stressed: this means that one of the syllables of the word (the only syllable in *eyes*!) is said with greater force, with greater effort, than the others; in *hardly* it is the first syllable /hɑːd-/, and in *believe* it is the second syllable /-liːv/. All the remaining syllables in the group are said more weakly; only /hɑːd-/, /-liːv/ and /aiz/ have this extra effort or *stress*. We can show this by placing the mark * immediately *before* the syllables which have stress, for example:

‖ai kud *hɑːdli bi*liːv mai *aiz‖

Hardly always has stress on the first syllable, never on the second, and *believe* always has stress on the second syllable, never on the first; every English word has a definite place for the stress and we are not allowed to change it. The first syllable is the most common place for the stress, as in *father, any, steadily, gathering, excellently, obstinacy, reasonableness*; many words are stressed on the second syllable, like *about, before, attractive, beginning, intelligent, magnificently*. Some words have *two* stressed syllables, for example, *fourteen* *fɔː*tiːn, *half-hearted* *hɑːf *hɑːtid, *disbelieve* *disbi*liːv, *contradiction* *kɔntrə*dikʃən, *qualification* *kwɔlifi*keiʃən, *examination* ig*zæmi*neiʃən, *terrified* *teri*faid, *intensify* in*tensi*fai.

There is no simple way of knowing which syllable or syllables in an English word must be stressed, but every time you learn another word you must be sure to learn how it is stressed: any good dictionary of English will give you this information. If you stress the wrong syllable it spoils the shape of the word for an English hearer and he may have difficulty in recognizing the word.

As we saw in the group *I could hardly believe my eyes* not all words are stressed; *I* and *could* and *my* are unstressed. What sort of words are stressed, then, and what sort are unstressed? First, all words of more than one syllable are stressed. In some circumstances English speakers do not stress such words, but it is always possible to stress them and you should do so. Next, words of one syllable are generally *not* stressed if they are purely grammatical words like pronouns (*I, me, you, he, she*, etc.), prepositions (*to, for, at, from, by*, etc.), articles (*the, a, an, some*). Other words are stressed, for example, full verbs (*eat, love, take, try*, etc.), nouns (*head, chair, book, pen*, etc.), adjectives (*good, blue, long, cold*, etc.), adverbs (*well, just, quite, not*) and the like. In general it is the picture words which are stressed, the words which give us the picture or provide most of the information. We shall see later that for special purposes it is possible to stress any English word, even the purely grammatical ones, but usually they are unstressed.

Syllables which are not stressed often contain the vowel /ə/ instead of any clearer vowel, and this vowel /ə/ only occurs in unstressed syllables, *never* in stressed ones. For instance, in all the examples on p. 106 the /ə/ is in an unstressed syllable. In the word *contain* kən*tein the second syllable is stressed and the first has /ə/, but in the noun *contents* *kɔntents the first syllable is stressed and has the clearer vowel /ɔ/. Here are some examples of the same kind; say them with the effort on the correct syllable and with the right vowels:

əb*tein	obtain	*ɔbdʒikt	object (n.)
pə*mit	permit (v.)	*pə:fikt	perfect (adj.)
prə*vaid	provide	*prougres	progress (n.)
*foutə*gra:f	photograph	fə*tɔgrəfi	photography
pri*pɛə	prepare	*prepə*reiʃən	preparation
kəm*bain	combine (v.)	*kɔmbi*neiʃən	combination
*kɔnvənt	convent	in*vent	invent

But it is not true, as you can see, that /ə/ is the only vowel which occurs in unstressed syllables; all the other vowels can occur there too and /i/ is commonly found there, the remaining vowels less commonly so. Here are examples of other vowels in unstressed syllables; say them as before:

*plenti	plenty	*eniθiŋ	anything
*hikʌp	hiccough	juː*tiliti	utility
*θæŋkju	thank you	*windou	window

trænz*leit	translate	mein*tein	maintain
di*said	decide	vai*breit	vibrate
ɔː*spiʃəs	auspicious	*gærɑːʒ	garage

WEAK FORMS OF WORDS

In *It was too expensive for them to buy* the words *too, expensive* and *buy* are stressed, giving it wəz *tuː ik*spensiv fə ðəm tə *bai. Notice the pronunciation of the words *was, for, them* and *to*; all of them have the vowel /ə/. If those words are pronounced alone, they have the pronunciations wɔz, fɔː, ðem and tuː, but usually they are not pronounced alone and usually they are not stressed, and then the forms with /ə/ are used; we call these the *weak forms* of those words.

English people often think that when they use these weak forms they are being rather careless in their speech and believe that it would be more correct always to use the strong forms, like wɔz, tuː, etc. This is not true, and English spoken with only strong forms sounds wrong. The use of weak forms is an essential part of English speech and you must learn to use the weak forms of 34 English words if you want your English to *sound* English. Some words have more than one weak form and the following list tells you when to use one and when the other:

Word	Weak form	Examples
and	ən	*blæk ən *wait.
as	əz	əz *gud əz *gould.
but	bət	bət *wai *nɔt?
than	ðən	*betə ðən *evə.
that	ðət	ai əd*mit ðət ai *did it.
		(The word *that* in phrases like *that man, that's good* is always pronounced ðæt and *never* weakened.)
he	iː	*did iː *win?

him	im	*giv im *tuː.
his	iz	ai *laik iz *tai.
her	əː	*teik əː *houm.
	(At the beginning of word groups the forms hiː, him, hiz, həː should be used: hiː *laiks it, həː *feis iz *red.)	
them	ðəm	*send ðəm bai *poust.
us	s (only in *let's*)	*lets *du: it *nau.
	əs	hi: *wount *let əs *du: it.
do	də	*hau də ðei *nou?
	(də is only used before consonants. Before vowels, use the strong form duː: *hau du: *ai *nou?)	
does	dəz	*wen dəz ðə *trein *liːv?
am	m (after *I*)	ai m *taiəd.
	əm (elsewhere)	*wen əm ai tə *bi: *ðɛə?
are	ə (before consonants)	ðə *gəːlz ə *bjuːtəfl̩.
	ər (before vowels)	ðə *men ər *ʌgli.
be	bi	*dount bi *ruːd.
is	s (after /p, t, k, f, θ/)	*ðæt s *fain.
	z (after vowels and voiced consonants except /z, ʒ, dʒ/)	*wɛə z *dʒɔn?
		*dʒɔn z *hiə.
	(After /s, z, ʃ, ʒ, tʃ, dʒ/ the strong form iz is always used: *witʃ iz *rait?)	
was	wəz	ðə *weðə wəz *terəbl̩!
has	əz (after /s, z, ʃ, ʒ, tʃ, dʒ/)	ðə *pleis əz *tʃeindʒd.
	s (after /p, t, k, f, θ/)	*dʒæk s *gɔn.
	z (elsewhere)	*dʒɔn z biːn *sik.
have	v (after *I, we, you, they*)	juː v *broukən it.
	əv (elsewhere)	ðə *men əv *gɔn.

had	d (after *I, he, she, we, you, they*)	ðei d *left *houm.
	əd (elsewhere)	ðə *dei əd biːn *fain.
	(At the beginning of word groups the forms hæz, hæv, hæd should be used: hæz *eniwʌn *found? When *has, have, had* are full verbs they should always be pronounced hæz, hæv, hæd: ai hæv *tuː *brʌðəz.)	
can	kən	*hau kən ai *help?
shall	ʃ|	ai ʃ| bi *krɔs.
will	l (after *I, he, she, we, you, they*)	ðei l *giv it ə*wei.
		(afer consonants, except /l/)	*ðis	*duː.
	əl (after vowels and /l/)	ðə *bɔi əl *luːz ən ðə *gəːl əl *win.
a	ə (before consonants)	ə *ʃiliŋ ə *dʌzn̩.
an	ən (before vowels)	*hæv ən *æp|.
the	ðə (before consonants)	ðə *mɔː ðə *meriə.
	(Before vowels the strong form ðiː should be used: ðiː *aːnts ən ðiː *ʌŋk|z.)	
some	səm	ai *niːd səm *peipə.
	(When *some* means 'a certain quantity' it is always stressed and therefore pronounced sʌm: *sʌm əv mai *frendz.)	
at	ət	*kʌm ət *wʌns.
for	fə (before consonants)	*kʌm fə *tiː.
	fər (before vowels)	*kʌm fər ə *miːl.
from	frəm	ai *sent it frəm *lʌndən.
of	əv	ðə *kwiːn əv *iŋglənd.

to   tə (before consonants)   tə *stei ɔː tə *gou.
       (Before vowels the strong
       form tuː should be used:
       ai *wɔntid tuː *aːsk juː.)

The word *not* has the weak forms /nt/ (after vowels) and /ṇt/ (after consonants) when it follows *are, is, should, would, has, have, could, dare, might.* Examples: ðei *aːnt *kʌmiŋ; hiː *hæzṇt ə*raivd. Notice especially the forms *can't* kaːnt, *shan't* ʃaːnt, *don't* dount, *won't* wount, *mustn't* mʌsṇt, in which *can, shall, do, will, must* are changed when they combine with *not.* Practise all the examples given here and be sure that the weak forms are really weak, then make up similar examples for yourself and practise those too.

THE USE OF STRONG FORMS

As I have said, the 34 common words which have weak forms also have strong forms, which *must* be used in the following cases:

1. Whenever the word is stressed, as it may be: *kæn ai?, *duː ðei?, *hæv juː *finiʃt?, juː məst *tʃuːz *ʌs ɔː *ðem, *hiː *laiks *hə: bət dəz *ʃiː *laik *him?

2. Whenever the word is *final* in the group: *dʒɔn hæz, *mɛəri wil, *juː aː, ai *dount *wɔnt tuː, *wɔts *ðæt fɔː?

Exceptions: he, him, his, her, them, us have their *weak* forms in final position (unless they are stressed of course): ai *tould əː, ʃiː *laiks ðəm, wiː *kɔːld fər im, ðei *laːft ət əs.

not has its weak form finally when attached to *can, have, is,* etc.: *dʒɔn *kaːnt, *mɛəri *izṇt; but never otherwise: ai *houp nɔt.

Some of the 34 words are very rarely either stressed or final in the group and so very rarely have their strong form, for example, *than, a, the.* But occasionally they are stressed for reasons of meaning and then they naturally have their strong form: ai sed *ei *sʌn, *nɔt *ðiː *sʌn (I said *a* son, not *the* sun).

Practise all these examples and then make up others for yourself and practise those too.

RHYTHM UNITS

Within the word group there is at least one stressed syllable (||*wen?|| ||*su:n|| ||*nau?|| ||*jes||). The length of the syllable in a very short 'group' of this kind depends on the natural length of the vowel and the following consonant(s), if any.

/nau/ is a very long syllable because it has a diphthong and no following consonant—we stretch it out.

/su:n/ is also very long because it has a long vowel followed by a weak consonant.

/wen/ is a little shorter because it has a short vowel, but not *very* short because of the slight lengthening effect of the following weak consonant.

/jes/ is the shortest of these syllables because it has a short vowel followed by a strong consonant, but notice that even this kind of syllable is not *very* short in English.

The stressed syllable may have one or more unstressed syllables before it:

||its *kould|| ||ai ə*gri:|| ||ai ʃ| kəm*plein||

These unstressed syllables before the stress are said very quickly, so they are all very short, as short as you can make them; but the stressed syllable is as long as before, so there is a great difference of length between the unstressed syllables and the stressed one. Say those examples with very quick, very short unstressed syllables, and then stretch out the stressed one. Do the same with these:

ai m *hiə	ai wəz *hiə	ai wəz in *hiə
ʃi:z *houm	ʃi:z ət *houm	bət ʃi:z ət *houm
ðei *wə:k	ðei kən *wə:k	ðei wər ət *wə:k
wi:l *si:	wi: ʃ| *si:	ən wi: ʃ| *si:

The stressed syllable may also be followed by one or more unstressed syllables:

‖*teik it‖   ‖*ɔːl əv it?‖   ‖*nætʃərəli‖

But these unstressed syllables are not said specially quickly; what happens is that the stressed syllable and the following unstressed syllable(s) share the amount of time which a single stressed syllable would have; so

*nain   *nainti   *naintiəθ

all take about the same time to say; nain is stretched out, but the nain in nainti is only half as long and the nain in naintiəθ is shorter still, and the unstressed syllables are of the same length as the stressed ones; these unstressed syllables *after* the stress must not be rushed, as the ones *before* the stress are, but must be given the same amount of time as the stressed syllable. Say those examples, and be sure that the three words all take about the same time to say. Then try these:

*gud	*betə	*eksələnt
*fain	*fainļ	*fainəli
*wil	*wiliŋ	*wiliŋnis
*wit	*witnis	*witnisiz
*driŋk	*driŋkiŋ	*driŋkiŋ it
*miːt	*miːtiŋ	*miːtiŋ ðəm

In the group ‖it wəz *betə‖ there are two unstressed syllables before the stress and one after it. The first two are said quickly, the last one not so quickly, taking the same amount of time as /be-/. Practise that group, with the first two syllables very short and the next two longer. Do the same with the following:

juː kən *siː ðəm   ai wəz in *lʌndən

ðei in*dʒɔid it   ʃiː ik*spektid it

hiː kud əv ə*vɔidid it   it wəz ə *mirək|

it wəz ən *æksidənt   mai ə*pɔlədʒiz

bət ðɛə wə *plenti əv ðəm   jɔːr im*pɔsəb|

The group ‖*wai *nɔt?‖ has two stresses and the two
syllables are given the same length. In ‖*wai *nɔt *gou?‖
the three stressed syllables are also equal in length. But in
‖*wai *nɔt *teik it?‖ the first two syllables *wai *nɔt are
equal in length but the following two syllables *teik it are
said in the same time as *wai, so they are both only half
the length of *wai and *nɔt. This is exactly what happens
with *nain and *nainti as we saw on p. 122. We could show
this as follows:

‖*w<u>ai</u>   *n<u>ɔt</u>‖   ‖*w<u>ai</u>   *n<u>ɔt</u>   *<u>gou</u>‖

‖*w<u>ai</u> *n<u>ɔt</u> *t<u>eik it</u>‖

Similarly in ‖*ðæts *kwait *pleznt‖ the two syllables of
*pleznt have the same amount of time as the single syllable
*ðæts or *kwait and are therefore only half as long.

‖*ð<u>æts</u> *kw<u>ait</u> *pl<u>ez</u><u>n̩t</u>‖

In ‖*dʒɔnz *eldist *sʌn‖ the stressed syllables *dʒɔnz and
*sʌn which are *not* followed by an unstressed syllable are of
the same length, and the two syllables of *eldist share this
same length of time between them.

‖*d<u>ʒɔnz</u> *<u>eld</u>ist *<u>sʌn</u>‖

In ‖*bouθ əv ðəm *keim *bæk‖ the *three* syllables *bouθ
əv ðəm are said in the same amount of time as *keim or
*bæk.

‖*b<u>ouθ</u> əv ðəm *<u>keim</u> *<u>bæk</u>‖

In ‖*bouθ əv ðəm *left *əːli‖ the three syllables of *bouθ
əv ðəm and the two syllables of *əːli are said in the same
amount of time as the single syllable *left, so *left is the

longest syllable, the two syllables of *ə:li are shorter and
the three of *bouθ əv ðəm are shorter still.

‖*bouθ əv ðəm *left *ə:li‖

A stressed syllable together with any unstressed syllables
which may follow it form a *stress group*. So *bouθ əv ðəm is
one stress group, *left is another and *ə:li is another. The
fundamental rule of English rhythm is this: *each stress group
within a word group is given the same amount of time.*

If we leave out any spaces between syllables belonging
to the same stress group it will remind us that they belong
to a single stress group and must be said in the same time
as other stress groups in the same word group:

‖*bouθəvðəm *left *ə:li‖

Do this for the following examples:

*let im *teik it	*send ðəm *leitə
*teik jɔ: *hæt ɔf	*nʌn əv əs *laikt it *ðɛə
*dount teik *tu: mʌtʃ *taim	*mei ai *bɔrou it *nau?
*iz ʃi: *gouiŋ ɔn *mʌndi?	*hæv ju: *hə:d hau *dʒɔn iz?
*wɔzņt it *wʌndəfli *kaind əv im?	*breik it intə *sevrəl *pi:siz

Now practise those examples; the best way is to beat
the rhythm with your hand, one beat for each stressed
syllable and with exactly the same time between each pair
of beats. I find it useful to bang rhythmically on the table
with my pen, and at each bang comes a stressed syllable;
you try it too. And don't forget that each stress group gets
the same time as the others in that word group, and that
each syllable in the stress group gets the same time as the
others in that stress group.

In the group ‖aim *gouiŋ *houm‖ there are two stress
groups *gouiŋ and *houm. The syllable aim does not
belong to any stress group since it comes *before* the stress,

and it is said very quickly, as we saw earlier, quicker than the unstressed syllable in the stress group *gouiŋ. We can show this as follows:

‖aim *gouiŋ *houm‖

In the group ‖aim *gouiŋ *houm tə*dei‖ the unstressed syllable /tə-/ in tə*dei behaves exactly like aim, it is said very quickly, and the stressed syllable *houm is still just as long as the two syllables of *gouiŋ, not reduced in length as you might expect:

‖aim *gouiŋ *houm tə*dei‖

So we say that /tə-/ does *not* belong to the same stress group as houm but that it is outside any stress group, like aim. Exactly the same is true for fə in ‖aim *gouiŋ *houm fə *krisməs‖

‖aim *gouiŋ *houm fə *krisməs‖

We say that these very quick, very short syllables come *before* the stress, and we might write these examples like this:

‖aim*gouiŋ *houm tə*dei‖
‖aim*gouiŋ *houm fə*krisməs‖

In this sort of arrangement any unstressed syllable *before* the stressed syllable is said very quickly and does not affect the length of syllables before it. We say them as quickly as we can so that they interfere as little as possible with the regular return of the stressed syllables. Any unstressed syllable *after* the stress is of course part of the stress group and shares the available time with the other syllables of the stress group.

A unit of this kind, with a stressed syllable as its centre and any unstressed syllables which may come *before* it and *after* it, is called a *rhythm unit*. So aim*gouiŋ is a rhythm unit, and so is *houm and so is fə*krisməs.

How do you decide what words or syllables go together in a rhythm unit? Here are the rules:

1. Any unstressed syllables at the beginning of a word group must go together with the following stress group:

||aiwəzin*lʌndən|| ||maiə*pɔlədʒiz||

2. If the unstressed syllable(s) is part of the same word as the stressed syllable they belong to the same rhythm group:

||*tʃiːpə *fɛəz|| ||*tʃiːp ə*fɛəz|| (cheaper fares, cheap affairs)

3. If the unstressed syllables are closely connected grammatically to the stressed word, although not a part of that word, they belong to the same rhythm unit:

||*givit tə*dʒɔn|| ||*teikðəm fərə*wɔːk||

||*hau didjuː*mænidʒ təbi*ðɛər in*taim?||

4. Whenever you are in doubt as to which rhythm unit unstressed syllables belong to, put them after a stress rather than before it. So in *He was older than me*, if you are doubtful about ðən, put it with ouldə and not with miː: ||hiːwəz*ouldəðən *miː||.

In many languages the rhythm unit is the syllable: each syllable has the same length as every other syllable and there are not the constant changes of syllable length which occur in English word groups. Some such languages are French, Spanish, Hindi, Yoruba. Speakers of these languages and others in which all the syllables have the same length will find English rhythm rather difficult, and they will need to work hard at it. If every syllable is made the same length in English it gives the effect of a machine-gun firing and makes the utterances very hard to understand.

Some good work on English rhythm will help greatly in improving the sound of your speech.

Practise the following examples, beating the rhythm of the stressed syllables as you go and varying the lengths of the syllables so as to keep the stress groups equal in length:

	*teikit *houm		*teikit tə*dʒɔn		*teikit tə*dʒɔnsən	
	*lait ðə*faiə		*laitiŋ ðə*faiə		hi:wəz*laitiŋ ðə*faiə	
	hi:wəz*moust ə*mju:ziŋ		hi:wəz*veri ə*mju:ziŋ	
	*dʒɔn wəz*leit		*dʒeni wəz*leit		*dʒenifə wəz*leit	
	hi:z*dʒʌst *ten		hi:z*dʒʌst *sevən		hi:z*dʒʌst *sevənti	
	itsə*ha:d *dʒɔb		itsə*triki *dʒɔb		itsə*difək	t *dʒɔb	
	itwəzə*riəli *gud *mi:l		itwəzə*riəli *plezn̩t *mi:l	
itwəzə*riəli *eksələnt *mi:l	
	hi:*pleiz *veri *wel		hi:z*pleiiŋ *veri *wel	
hi:z*pleiiŋit *veri *wel	
	ju:*didit *ra:ðə *wel		ju:*didit *ra:ðə *betə	
ju:*didit *ra:ðə *klevəli	
	ai*hævn̩t ə*paund *nout		ai*hævn̩t ə*ʃiliŋ *pi:s	
          ai*hævn̩t ə*θrepəni *bit||

FLUENCY

One other thing which you must pay attention to in saying word groups is that you say them *fluently, smoothly,* with no gaps or hesitations in the middle. When you know what words you have to say you should be capable of saying them without stumbling over the sounds and sequences of sounds. In English, as we have seen, one word is not separated from another by pausing or hesitating; the end of one word flows straight on to the beginning of the next. To improve your fluency try the method of lengthening word groups. Here is an example:

I went home – on the Sunday – morning – train.

First you say the short group *I went home*—smoothly; if you stumble, say it again, until you are sure that you can do it. Then add the next three words and say *I went home on the Sunday*, also without stumbling. Now add *morning* and say the whole thing from the beginning; and finally add *train*. Don't be satisfied until you can say it without hesitation and with your best English sounds and rhythm. Other examples for practice are on p. 135.

One difficulty which often affects foreign learners is connected with a vowel at the beginning of words, especially if it begins a stressed syllable. An example is: *He's always asking awkward questions* where *ɔːlwiz, *aːskiŋ and *ɔːkwəd all begin with a stressed vowel. English speakers glide smoothly from the final sound of the word before to the initial vowel of the following word with no break, no hesitation. Many speakers of other languages separate the two words by a glottal stop (see p. 19) and this gives a very jerky effect in English. You must try to go smoothly and continuously from one word to the other, with no glottal stop, no break.

‖hiːz *ɔːlwiz *aːskiŋ *ɔːkwəd *kwestʃənz‖

When the final sound of the word before is a consonant it will help if you imagine that it belongs to the following word, and we might transcribe our example: ‖hiː *zɔːlwi *zaːski *ŋɔːkwəd *kwestʃənz‖. This will stop you making a gap before the vowel.

If the final sound of the word before is a vowel there are various ways of avoiding the gap. In ðiː *ʌðə it may help to write a little j before the /ʌ/: ðiː *ʲʌðə. The glide from iː to ʌ is very like a j but a very gentle one. The same trick can be used after /i/ and the diphthongs /ei, ai, ɔi/ which end in /i/. ðei *ʲaː, mai *ʲaːnt, ðə bɔi *ʲet it (*they are, my aunt, the boy ate it*). However, we do distinguish between *my ears* and *my years*, etc., mai *ⁱiəz and mai *jiəz, where jiəz has a longer and stronger j than the short and gentle glide before iəz.

Similarly, after /uː/ and the diphthongs /ou, au/ which end in u, we can use a little w-sound as the link, for example *two others*, *tuː *ʷʌðəz, *go in* *gou *ʷin, *how odd* *hau *ʷɔd. Again we distinguish between *two-eyed* and *too wide*: *tuː *ʷaid, *tuː *waid.

The vowels /əː/ and /ə/ can always be linked to a following vowel by /r/: *her own* həːr *oun, *for ever* fər *evə, and this is also true for /iə, ɛə, uə/: *clear air* *kliər *ɛə, *share out* *ʃɛər *aut, *poor Eve!* *puər *iːv. Again it may help to attach the r to the following word: həː *ʳoun, *kliə *ʳɛə, etc. When /ɔː/ or /ɑː/ occur at the end of a word and a vowel immediately follows we also use /r/ as a link if the spelling has the letter *r* in it, but not otherwise, so /r/ occurs in *more and more* *mɔː *ʳən *mɔː but not in *saw off* *sɔː *ɔf, and it occurs in *far away* *fɑː *ʳə*wei but not in *Shah of Persia* *ʃɑː əv *pəːʃə (see p. 79). When we go from /ɔː/ or /ɑː/ to a following vowel without a linking /r/ we glide smoothly from one to the other with no interruption of the voice by a glottal stop. Other examples for practice are on page 135.

CHANGING WORD-SHAPES

We have already seen that some words have weak and strong forms depending on their place in the group and on stress. The shape of a word may also be altered by nearby sounds; normally we pronounce *one* as wʌn, but *one more* may be pronounced wʌm mɔː, where the shape of *one* has changed because of the following /m/ in *more*. Also *next* is usually pronounced nekst, but in *next month* may be neks mʌnθ, where the final /t/ has disappeared.

Alterations like wʌm mɔː where one phoneme replaces

another mainly affect the alveolar sounds /t, d, n, s, z/ when they are final in the word:

Before /p, b, m/   /p/ replaces /t/:

right place	raip pleis
white bird	waip bəːd
not me	nɔp miː

/b/ replaces /d/:

hard path	hɑːb pɑːθ
good boy	gub bɔi
good morning	gub mɔːniŋ

/m/ replaces /n/:

gone past	gɔm pɑːst
gone back	gɔm bæk
ten men	tem men

Before /k, g/   /k/ replaces /t/:

white coat	waik kout
that girl	ðæk gəːl

/g/ replaces /d/:

bad cold	bæg kould
red gate	reg geit

/ŋ/ replaces /n/:

one cup	wʌŋ kʌp
main gate	meiŋ geit

Similarly, the sequences /nt/ and /nd/ may be replaced by /mp/ or /ŋk/ and /mb/ or /ŋg/ in *plant pot* plɑːmp pɔt, *stand back* stæmb bæk, *plant carrots* plɑːŋk kærəts, *stand guard* stæŋg gɑːd. Even the sequences /dṇt/ and /tṇd/ may be completely altered in a similar way in *couldn't come* kugŋk kʌm, *frightened girl* fraikŋg gəːl.

Before /ʃ, j/   /ʃ/ replaces /s/:

	nice shoes	naiʃ ʃuːz
	this year	ðiʃ jiə
/ʒ/ replaces /z/:	those shops	ðouʒ ʃɔps
	where's yours	wɛəʒ jɔːz

None of these alterations is necessary, so although you will hear English people use them, especially when they speak quickly, you need not imitate them.

In another kind of alteration the strong consonant of a pair replaces the weak consonant in compound words like *fivepence* faifpəns and *newspaper* njuːspeipə and in the closely connected *I have to*, *he has to*: ai hæf tuː, hiː hæs tuː. You should use these pronunciations, but do not make it a general rule to replace the weak consonant by the strong in other cases; you must distinguish between *the price ticket* and *the prize ticket*: ðə prais tikit, ðə praiz tikit. Notice too that the English do *not* replace the strong consonant by the weak in phrases like *black box*, *great day*, which must be pronounced blæk bɔks, greit dei and *not* blæg bɔks, greid dei.

Some of the alterations mentioned here have taken place in the past inside English words, leaving them with a shape which is now normal. Examples are: *handkerchief* hæŋkə-tʃiːf, *special* speʃl, *soldier* souldʒə; you must use these forms, but there are others which you may hear which are not essential though you can use them if you wish. Examples are: *admirable* æbmərəbl, *Watkins* wɔkkinz, *broadcast* brɔːg-kaːst, *utmost* ʌpmoust, *inmate* immeit.

Disappearances of sounds, as in neks dei, most often affect /t/ when it is final in a word after /s/ or /f/ (as in *last* or *left*) and the following word begins with a stop, nasal or friction sound.

/st/ + stop:
last time	laːs taim	fast bus	faːs bʌs

+ nasal:
best man	bes mæn	first night	fəːs nait

+ friction:
West side	wes said	best friend	bes frend

/ft/ + stop:

    lift boy   lif bɔi   stuffed chicken stʌf tʃikin

  + nasal:

    soft mattress sɔf mætrəs left knee   lef niː

  + friction:

    left shoe   lef ʃuː   soft snow   sɔf snou

The /t/ in /st, ft/ may also disappear when other consonants follow, but this is less common. Examples are: *last lap* lɑːs læp, *next week* neks wiːk, *best road* bes roud, *left leg* lef leg, *soft rain* sɔf rein, *soft water* sɔf wɔːtə.

The /d/ in /nd/ or /md/ often disappears if the following word begins with a nasal or weak stop consonant:

/nd/ + nasal:	blind man	blain mæn
	kind nurse	kain nəːs
+ weak stop:	tinned bacon	tin beikən
	stand guard	stæn gɑːd
/md/ + nasal:	skimmed milk	skim milk
	he seemed nice	hiː siːm nais
+ weak stop:	it seemed good	it siːm gud
	he climbed back	hiː klaim bæk

The /d/ in /nd, md/ may also disappear when other consonants follow, but this is less common. Examples: *blind chance* blain tʃɑːns, *send seven* sen sevən, *hand-woven* hæn wouvən, *he blamed them* hiː bleim ðəm, *she seemed well* ʃiː siːm wel, *a framed picture* ə freim piktʃə.

When /t/ or /d/ occur between two other stop consonants they are never heard and you should leave them out, for example: *locked car* lɔk kɑː, *strict parents* strik pɛərənts, *he stopped behind* hiː stɔp bihaind, *dragged back* dræg bæk, *rubbed down* rʌb daun. It is not *necessary* for you to use any of the other reduced forms mentioned above, but if you find it easier to do so you may use the more common ones.

Similar disappearances have taken place in the past in-side English words, leaving them with a shape which is now normal. Examples are: *grandmother* grænmʌðə, *handsome* hænsəm, *castle* kɑːsl̩, *postman* pousmən, *draughtsman* drɑːfs-mən. In all these cases you should use this normal form. There are other cases where two forms may be heard: *often* ɔfn̩, ɔftən; *kindness* kainnis, kaindnis; *asked* ɑːst, ɑːskt; *clothes* klouz, klouðz; and you can use whichever you find easiest.

Vowels have often disappeared from English words in the past, leaving a form which is the normal one, for example: *family* fæmli, *garden* gɑːdn̩, *Edinburgh* edn̩brə, *awful* ɔːfl̩, *evil* iːvl̩, *interest* intrəst, *history* histri. You should naturally use these normal forms. In other cases there are two possi-bilities, for example: *generous* dʒenrəs, dʒenərəs; *pattern* pætən, pætn̩; *deliberate* dilibrət, dilibərət; *probably* prɔbbli, prɔbəbli; *properly* prɔpli, prɔpəli. In these and similar cases it is best for you to use the longer form.

All these examples of changes and disappearances of sounds should encourage you to listen most carefully to the *real* shapes of English words, which are so often different from the shapes which the ordinary spelling might suggest. You can always find the normal shape of a word by looking for it in a pronouncing dictionary, for instance Daniel Jones's *English Pronouncing Dictionary*, which is most useful for any foreign user of English, but the most important thing, as always, is to use your ears and really *listen* to English as it is.

EXERCISES ON CHAPTER 6

1. Divide the following passage into word groups (p. 114).

I have needed some new bookshelves for a long time. So during my holiday I decided to tackle the job myself. Not that I am very clever with my hands but it did not seem too difficult and as I had already said that we could not afford to go away I thought it would be prudent not to spend money having it done professionally. I bought the wood at the local handicraft shop, and I had plenty of screws, but I found that my old saw, which had been left behind by the previous owner of the house, was not good enough and I decided to buy a new one. That was my first mistake, my second was to go to the biggest ironmonger in London and ask for a saw. You would think it was simple, wouldn't you, to buy a saw. But it is not. I said to the man behind the counter, 'I want a saw.' He was a nice man and did his best for me. 'Yes, sir, what kind of saw?' 'Oh, a saw for cutting wood.' 'Yes, sir, but we have fifteen different kinds for different jobs. What did you want it for?' I explained about my bookshelves, and felt like an ignorant fool in a world of experts, which was true. He saw that I was a novice and was very kind. He told me what I should need and advised me to have a ladies' size. 'Easier to manage for the beginner, sir.' He was not being nasty just helpful and I was grateful to him. He also sold me a book on woodwork for schoolboys and I've been reading it with great interest. The next time I am on holiday I shall start on the shelves.

2. Each of the following examples contains one or more of the words which often have weak forms (p. 117). Transcribe the examples phonetically, showing the stressed syllables and the weak (or strong!) forms of those words:

They came to the door.	There were two of them.
What are you surprised at?	She is as old as the hills.
She has an uncle and a cousin.	I shall be angry.
Who will meet him at the air-port?	I will.

What is her phone number?	What does that matter?
I would like some tea.	Well, make some.
What has John come for?	For his saw that you borrowed.
What can I do?	More than I can.
He was pleased, wasn't he?	Of course he was.
When am I going to get it?	I am not sure.
I have taken it from the shelf.	Yes, I thought you had.
They had already read it.	But so had I.

3. Mark the words in the passage in Exercise 1 which should have a weak form.

4. Use the following lengthening word groups for practising fluency (p. 127):

I don't know – how – long – I need – to wait – for John – to come – home.

It was near the end – of the week – before – I arrived – back – from Scotland.

Who was that – awful woman – you talked to – all evening – at the party?

I can't understand – how you did it – so quickly – and efficiently, – Mr Southwood.

When did you hear – that story – about John – and the girl – next door?

Come and have dinner – with us – on Thursday – the twenty-third – of this month.

5. Use the following for practice in smoothness with initial vowels (p. 128):

I was better off on my own.

Don't argue with anyone as old as I am.

How awful it is to be ill when everyone else is all right.

The hungrier I am, the more I eat.

Is there any flaw in my argument, Oscar?

Have you ever asked Ann about Arthur and Amy?
I owe everything I am to my uncle and aunt.
Come over to our house for an evening.
I haven't set eyes on Alec for ages and ages.
I ended up owing eighty-eight pounds.
You always ought to earn an honest living.

6. Arrange each word group in the passage in Exercise 1 into one or more rhythm units showing the stressed syllable and the unstressed syllables attached to it.

7. Which words in the passage might show *alterations* or *disappearances* in sounds (pp. 129 and 131)?

8. Transcribe the whole passage phonetically showing word groups, stressed syllables, rhythm groups and weak forms of words; then compare it with the version on p. 164 and notice any differences. Practise each word group aloud, concentrating on smoothness and rhythm.

7

INTONATION

Every language has melody in it; no language is spoken on the same musical note all the time. The voice goes up and down and the different pitches of the voice combine to make tunes. In some languages the tune mainly belongs to the *word*, being part of its shape, and if the tune of the word is wrong its shape is spoiled. The Chinese languages are like this and so are many others in South-east Asia, Africa and America. In these languages the same sounds said with different tunes may make quite different words: in Mandarin Chinese maː said with level pitch means *mother* but maː with a rise in pitch means *horse*, an important difference! In many other languages, of which English is one, the tune belongs not to the word but to the word group. If you say the English word *No* with different tunes it is still the same word, but nevertheless tune plays an important part in English. We can say a word group definitely or we can say it hesitantly, we can say it angrily or kindly, we can say it with interest or without interest, and these differences are largely made by the tunes we use: the words do not change their meaning but the tune we use adds something to the words, and what it adds is the speaker's feelings at that moment; this way of using tunes is called *intonation*.

English intonation is *English*: it is not the same as the intonation of any other language. Some people imagine that intonation is the same for all languages, but this is not true. You must learn the *shapes* of the English tunes, and these may be quite different from the normal tunes of your own language; and you must learn the *meanings* of the

English tunes too, because they are important. For example, *thank you* may be said in two ways: in the first the voice starts high and ends low, and this shows real gratitude; in the second the voice starts low and ends high, and this shows a rather casual acknowledgement of something not very important. A bus conductor will say *thank you* in this second way when he collects your money and this is quite reasonable since he does not feel great gratitude. But if an English friend invites you to spend a week-end at his home and you reply with the second *thank you* instead of the first your friend will be offended because you don't sound really grateful. You may have made an honest mistake but it is difficult for him to realize that; he will think that you are being impolite.

TUNE SHAPES

The shape of a tune is decided partly by the number of important words in the group and partly by the exact attitude you wish to express. What do we mean by 'important words'? These are the words which carry most of the meaning in a word group: for example, suppose that in answer to the question *How was John?* you say: *He was in an appallingly bad temper*. The first four words are not specially helpful to the meaning, not important, but the last three words *are* important; each of them adds quite a lot to the picture you are giving of John. Let's see how it might be said.

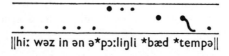

||hiː wəz in ən ə*pɔːliŋli *bæd *tempə||

This diagram shows the approximate height of the voice on each syllable: the first five syllables have low pitch;

then there is a jump to the stressed syllable of *appallingly* (marked with a big dot) and the next two syllables are on the same rather high pitch; then *bad* is a little lower and *temper* glides downwards from the stressed to the unstressed syllable.

Notice that there are three changes of pitch connected with stressed syllables. This shows that these words are important. An important word *always* has a stressed syllable and usually has a change of pitch connected to it.

Now suppose that the question is *Was John in a good temper?* In this case *temper* occurs in the question so that in the answer it is not specially important, it doesn't add anything to the picture, it gives little information; and the tune shows this:

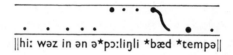

||hi: wəz in ən ə*pɔ:liŋli *bæd *tempə||

Now there are only *two* changes of pitch, connected with the stressed syllables of *appallingly* and *bad*. So these two words are still marked as important, but *temper* is not. Although it still has the first syllable stressed, the fact that there is no change of pitch shows that the speaker is not treating it as important.

Lastly, suppose that the question is *Was John in a bad temper?* *Bad* and *temper* are not important in the answer because both are already in the questioner's mind, so the speaker says:

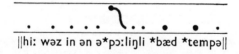

||hi: wəz in ən ə*pɔ:liŋli *bæd *tempə||

Both *bad* and *temper* are still stressed, but they are shown to be unimportant because they have no change of pitch. Important words are not the same as stressed words. Stressed words may not be important, though important words *must* be stressed. It is not only the normally stressed words, like *appallingly* and *bad* and *temper* in our example, which may be felt to be important by the speaker; *any* word may be important if the situation makes it important. For example, if the first speaker refuses to believe in John's bad temper and says *He can't have been in an appallingly bad temper*, then our example would be:

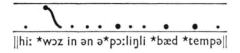

||hiː *wɔz in ən ə*pɔːliŋli *bæd *tempə||

Here the word *was* which is not usually stressed at all has both the stress and change of pitch which mark it as important, indeed as the only really important word in the group; and notice that when it is stressed it has its strong form.

In answer to the question *What is John like?* we might reply: *He seems very nice* and the usual way of saying this is:

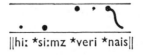

||hiː *siːmz *veri *nais||

Here *seems* is not marked as important; even though it is stressed it is on a low pitch like the unimportant initial words in our first example; the meaning of the group is approximately the same as *He's very nice*. But if it is:

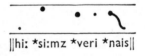

||hiː *siːmz *veri *nais||

there is much more weight in *seems* because of the jump in pitch, and we understand that the speaker considers it important: he does so in order to emphasize that he is talking about the *seeming*, the *appearance*, and is not saying that John really *is* very nice.

So the important words in a group affect the shape of a tune. Now look at the following:

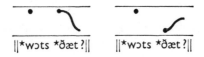

||*wɔts *ðæt?|| ||*wɔts *ðæt?||

In both these examples the words *what* and *that* are marked as important; *what* is stressed and on a high pitch and *that* has a fall in pitch in the first case and a rise in the second. So it is not only the number of important words which affects the tune-shape. The difference here is a difference of attitude in the speaker; the first example is a rather serious, business-like question, the second shows rather more interest and friendliness. So the attitude of the speaker, his feelings as he says the group, affects the tune-shape, and affects it very much, as we shall see.

Before we think about the speaker's attitudes let's see what tunes you must learn to use in speaking English: I cannot teach you *all* the tunes that English speakers use, but I shall describe the ones you *must* know to make your English sound like English.

THE FALLING TUNE—THE GLIDE-DOWN

In the shortest word-groups, where we use just one important word, the falling tune consists of a fall in the voice from a fairly high pitch to a very low one. The fall is on the stressed syllable or from the stressed syllable to a following one:

||*nou|| ||*tu:|| ||*tenpəns|| ||*eksələnt|| ||*definitli||

Notice. 1. On a single syllable the voice falls within the syllable.

2. On more than one syllable the voice either falls within the stressed syllable or it jumps down from that syllable to the next.

3. Unstressed syllables at the end are all very low.

Start with *tenpəns and start by *singing* it—it doesn't matter if your singing is not very good, it will be good enough for this! Sing the first syllable on a fairly high note, but not *very* high. I cannot tell you exactly what note to sing because I don't know whether you have a naturally high voice or a naturally low one, but sing a note rather above the middle of your voice. Then sing the second syllable on the lowest possible note—growl it! Do this several times and hear the fall in pitch, then gradually go more quickly and stop singing. Say it, but with the same tune as before. Do the same with *eksələnt and *definitli, and be sure that the unstressed syllables are as low as possible. Don't let them rise at the end; keep growling!

If there are other words following the fall they may still have stress, as in our previous example:

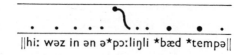

||hi: wəz in ən ə*pɔ:liŋli *bæd *tempə||

But they are still said on that very low pitch, just like the unstressed syllables. Keep them right down.

Now try *nou. Sing it on two notes, the high one, then the low one, as if it had two syllables, and again increase your speed and stop singing, but keep the same tune.

Be sure that you finish with the pitch as low as you possibly can, right down in your boots!

When there is more than one important word in the group, the last one has the fall but the others are treated differently:

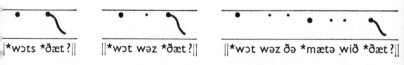

|*wɔts *ðæt?|| ||*wɔt wəz *ðæt?|| ||*wɔt wəz ðə *mætə ˌwið *ðæt?||

Notice. 1. The stressed syllable of the first important word is high and any unstressed syllables following it are on the same pitch.

2. The stressed syllable of the second important word is a little lower and any unstressed syllables following it are on the same pitch.

3. The fall starts at the same pitch as the syllable just before it.

In groups with more than three important words the stressed syllable of each one is lower than the one before; this is why we call the tune the Glide-Down:

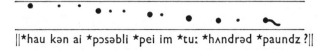

||*hau kən ai *pɔsəbli *pei im *tu: *hʌndrəd *paundz?||

Start with *wɔts said on a rather high pitch in your voice; keep the voice level, don't let it rise or fall. Then add *ðæt with the same fall as before. Then put wəz between the two, at the same level as *wɔt and the beginning of *ðæt; don't let it be higher or lower than *wɔt. If necessary start by singing it. Then try *wɔt wəz ðə *mætə wið *ðæt in three parts: *wɔt wəz ðə all on the high note, then *mætə wið all a little lower; put them together: *wɔt wəz ðə *mætə wið to form a high step followed by a lower step. Then add *ðæt, falling as before from the same pitch

143

as wið. Similarly practise the longest example in parts, each part a little lower than the one before, and the fall at the end from the pitch of the syllable before. Try to keep the unstressed syllables on the same pitch as the stressed ones, and not to let them jump either up or down. This treatment of the important words in downward 'steps' occurs also in other tunes, as we shall see later.

If there are any unstressed syllables before the stressed syllable of the first important word, these are all said on a rather low pitch:

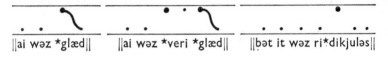

||ai wəz *glæd|| ||ai wəz *veri *glæd|| ||bət it wəz ri*dikjuləs||

Also, any stressed syllable near the beginning which belongs to a word which is not important is said on this same rather low pitch:

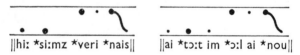

||hi: *si:mz *veri *nais|| ||ai *tɔ:t im *ɔ:l ai *nou||

Notice. These low syllables at the beginning are not at the lowest possible pitch like the ones at the end, but they must be lower than the high pitch which follows.

Practise these examples and be sure that the voice jumps upwards from the low syllables at the beginning to the first high-pitched stress.

We have a way of showing the Glide-Down which is simpler and quicker than the dots and lines used up to now. Before the stressed syllable where the voice falls we put ('). So: ||`nou|| ||`tu:|| ||`tenpəns|| ||`eksələnt|| ||`definitli||. Notice that no other mark is needed to show the very low unstressed syllables at the end—any unstressed syllables after a fall are *always* low.

Before the stressed syllable of each other important word we put ('). So: ‖'wɔts ˎðæt‖ ‖'wɔt wəz ˎðæt‖ ‖'wɔt wəz ðə 'mætə wið ˎðæt‖ ‖'hau kən ai 'pɔsəbli 'pei im 'tu: 'hʌndrəd ˎpaundz‖. Each of these marks shows a step, beginning with a high one and gradually coming lower until the fall is reached.

Unstressed syllables at the beginning have no mark before them: ‖ai wəz ˎglæd‖ ‖ai wəz 'veri ˎglæd‖ ‖bət it wəz riˎdikjuləs‖. If there is a low-pitched stress near the beginning (as in hi: *si:mz *veri *nais) it is marked by (ˌ); so: ‖hi: ˌsi:mz 'veri ˎnais‖ ‖ai ˌtɔːt im 'ɔːl ai ˎnou‖. And the same mark is used for stressed syllables which come after the fall. So ‖hi: wəz in ən əˋpɔːliŋli ˌbæd ˌtempə‖.

So with these few marks we can show all the features of the Glide-Down. In the following examples, first write them out in the longer way with dots and lines, to make sure you understand what the simpler system means, then practise them carefully:

‖ˎteik it‖ ‖ˎhæv ðəm‖ ‖ˎsplendid‖ ‖ˎnɔnsəns‖ ‖ˎwʌndəf‖‖
‖ˎdʒɔnz ˌkʌmiŋ‖ ‖ˎsu:zənz ˌnɔkiŋ ət ðə ˌdɔ:‖ ‖ˎten‖ ‖ˎtu:‖
‖ˎfaiv‖ ‖ˎeit‖ ‖ˎsiks‖ ‖ˎhɑ:f‖ ‖ˎðis‖ ‖ˎwitʃ‖ ‖ˎfɔ: ˋʃiliŋz‖
‖ˎfifti ˎpaundz‖ ‖ˎsevənti ˎfaiv‖ ‖ˎwʌn ən ə ˎhɑ:f‖ ‖it wəz imˎpɔsəb‖‖ ‖ai kud əv ˎkraid‖ ‖ðei wər in ə 'terəb‖ ˎmes‖
‖ai l 'si: ju: ɔn 'θə:zdi ˎnait‖ ‖its 'dʒʌst 'ɑ:ftə ˎmidnait‖ ‖ðɛə wə 'tu: 'meni ˎpi:p‖ ˌðɛə‖ ‖ˎwai did ju: 'tel im i: wəz ˋrɔŋ?‖
‖it ˌwɔznt 'hɑ:f əz 'difik‖t əz ai ˋθɔ:t it ˌwud bi:‖ ‖ju: kən ˌfoun mi: 'eni 'taim əv ðə 'dei ɔ: ˎnait‖ ‖ai ˌweitid ˌɔ:lmoust 'twenti 'faiv ˎminits fə ðə ˌretʃid ˌmæn‖.

THE FIRST RISING TUNE—THE GLIDE-UP

The Glide-Up is just like the Glide-Down except that it ends with a rise in the voice instead of a fall. Both important and unimportant words before the rise are treated exactly as in the Glide-Down. An example is *But is it true that you're changing your job?*

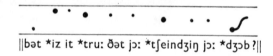

||bət *iz it *tru: ðət jɔ: *tʃeindʒiŋ jɔ: *dʒɔb?||

The last important word is *job* and here the voice rises from a low pitch to one just above the middle of the voice. Apart from this the tune is the same as in the Glide-Down: the unstressed syllable at the beginning is low, and there is a step at the stressed syllable of each important word.

Similarly, *Are you married?* would be:

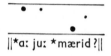

||*ɑ: ju: *mærid?||

Notice that the stressed syllable of the last important word is low and that the voice jumps up to the unstressed syllable. And notice too that in *Have you posted it to him?* we have:

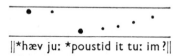

||*hæv ju: *poustid it tu: im?||

where again the stressed syllable of the last important word is low and each following unstressed syllable is a little higher, the last one of all being on the same fairly high note as in the previous examples.

Once again there may be stressed words within the rise, but they are not felt to be important:

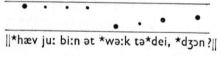

||*hæv ju: bi:n ət *wə:k tə*dei, *dʒɔn?||

Work is the last important word, and although *today* and *John* are stressed they behave just like the unstressed syllables of the last example and are not considered important by the speaker.

Practise with the following:

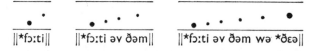

||*fɔːti|| ||*fɔːti əv ðəm|| ||*fɔːti əv ðəm wə *ðɛə||

The first syllable must be low, and the last syllable fairly high; concentrate on these and let any syllables between these points take care of themselves. How you get from the low to the higher note at the end doesn't matter, but be sure that you start low and end fairly high (not *very* high!).

Now try the rise on one syllable:

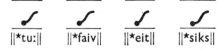

||*tuː|| ||*faiv|| ||*eit|| ||*siks||

If necessary sing the two notes as if there were two syllables and then gradually speed up and stop singing. Notice that the rise is slower on a long syllable like *tuː or *faiv, quicker on *eit where the diphthong is shortened, and quickest on *siks where the vowel is shortest.

Now try adding other important words before the rise; say them as you did in the Glide-Down:

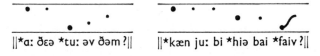

||*ɑː ðɛə *tuː əv ðəm?|| ||*kæn juː biː *hiə bai *faiv?||

And get the voice down low for the beginning of the rise.

In the simpler intonation marking, we use (,) before the stressed syllable of the last important word to show where the rise starts and (·) before any stressed syllable within the rise. The other marks are the same as for the Glide-Down. So the examples used in this section are marked as follows:

‖bət 'iz it 'tru: ðət jɔ: 'tʃeindʒiŋ jɔ: ˌdʒɔb?‖   ‖'ɑ: ju: ˌmærid?‖
‖'hæv ju: ˌpoustid it tu: im?‖   ‖'hæv ju: bi:n ət ˌwə:k tə·dei
·dʒɔn?‖   ‖ˌfɔ:ti‖   ‖ˌfɔ:ti əv ðəm‖   ‖ˌfɔ:ti əv ðəm wə ·ðɛə‖
‖ˌtu:‖   ‖ˌfaiv‖   ‖ˌeit‖   ‖ˌsiks‖   ‖'ɑ: ðɛə ˌtu: əv ðəm?‖   ‖'kæn
ju: bi 'hiə bai ˌfaiv?‖

Compare these with the fuller marking on the previous pages, then write out the fuller marking for the examples below and finally practise them carefully:

‖'hu:z ˌðæt?‖   ‖'dount bi ˌlɔŋ‖   ‖'giv it tə ˌmi:‖   ‖aim 'dʒʌst
ˌkʌmiŋ‖   ‖iz 'eniθiŋ ðə ˌmætə?‖   ‖kən 'eniwʌn 'tel mi: ðə
ˌtaim?‖   ‖ai wəz 'ounli 'traiiŋ tə ˌhelp‖   ‖ju: kən 'si: it ə'gen
təˌmɔrou‖   ‖hi:z 'pə:fiktli 'keipəbḷ əv 'lukiŋ 'ɑ:ftər imˌself‖
‖ai ˌtould im ai wəz 'veri 'pli:zd tə ˌsi: im‖   ‖ai ʃɑ:nt bi:
'eni 'leitə ðən ai ˌju:ʒuəli ·æm‖   ‖'did ju: 'sei it wəz jɔ:
ˌtwentiəθ ·bə:θdi tə·dei?‖   ‖'kud ai 'bɔrou 'ðis ˌbuk fər ə ·dei
ɔ: ·tu:?‖   ‖'wud ju: 'maind if ai 'brɔ:t mai ˌmʌðər in ·lɔ: tə
·si: ju:?‖

THE SECOND RISING TUNE—THE TAKE-OFF

After the Glide-Down and the Glide-Up we have the Take-Off; this also ends with a rise in the voice, like the Glide-Up, but any words and syllables before the rise are low. An example is:

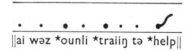

‖ai wəz *ounli *traiiŋ tə *help‖

We call it the Take-Off because, like an aeroplane taking off, it starts by running along at a low level and finally rises into the air.

The rise, as in the Glide-Up, either takes place on one syllable, like *help*, or it is spread over several syllables:

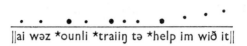

||ai wəz *ounli *traiiŋ tə *help im wið it||

Before the rise any stressed word is felt to be important, even though there is no change of pitch. All the syllables before the rise are said on the same low pitch as the beginning of the rise; they must not be higher than this, or you will have a Glide-Up instead of a Take-Off.

Practise the following and concentrate on keeping the syllables up to and including the beginning of the rise on the same low pitch:

||it *wɔz|| ||ai wəz *traiiŋ|| || juː *didṇt *riəli *həːt jɔː*self||

In the simpler intonation marking the rise has the same mark as before (ˌ), any stressed syllables *after* this have (·), and any stressed syllables *before* it have (ˌ). So our examples are marked:

	ai wəz ˌounli ˌtraiiŋ tə ˌhelp	
	ai wəz ˌounli ˌtraiiŋ tə ˌhelp im wið it	
|it ˌwɔz|| ||ai wəz ˌtraiiŋ|| ||juː ˌdidṇt ˌriəli ˌhəːt jɔː·self|

Practise the following examples and be sure to keep the syllables before the rise low:

	juː ˌlaikt it				juː in,dʒɔid it				juː wər in,dʒɔiiŋ it	
	ai ˌdidṇt ˌhəːt juː				ˌnouwʌnz ˌstɔpiŋ juː	
	it wəz ˌpəːfiktli ˌʌndəˌstændəbḷ	
	ai ˌwɔzṇt ikˌspektiŋ im ət ˌsiks ə ˌklɔk in ðə ˌmɔːniŋ	
	ai ˌdidṇt ˌθiŋk hiːd ˌmaind miː ˌbɔrouiŋ it fər ə ˌwail	
	juː ˌʃudṇt əv ˌgivən im ˌɔːl ðæt ˌmʌni, juː ·sili ·bɔi	

THE FALLING-RISING TUNE—THE DIVE

The last of our tunes that you must learn is the Dive. In its shortest form this consists of a fall from rather high to low and then a rise to about the middle of the voice.

This fall-rise is connected with the stressed syllable of the last important word, like the fall and the rise of the other tunes. But it is only completed on one syllable if that syllable is final in the group. If there is one or several syllables following, the fall and the rise are separated:

The fall is on the stressed syllable of the last important word and the rise on the last syllable of all. In the following examples:

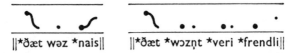

there are stressed (but not important) words following the fall; in that case the rise at the end is from the last of the stressed syllables.

Words or syllables before the fall are said in the same way as for the Glide-Down and Glide-Up. Examples:

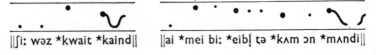

Notice that the fall of the fall-rise is always from a fairly high note.

If the stressed syllable of the last important word is final in the group, or if it is followed only by unstressed syllables, we put (ᵛ) before it in the simpler intonation marking, so:

‖ᵛfaiv‖ ‖ᵛwai‖ ‖ᵛsuːn‖ ‖ᵛtwenti‖ ‖ᵛsevənti‖ ‖ᵛsevənti əv ðəm‖.

But if the fall is followed by one or more stressed syllables we mark the fall with (ˋ) and we put (ˌ) before the last stressed syllable of all; any other stressed syllables have (ˌ) before them. So:

‖ˋðæt wəz ˌnais‖ ‖ˋðæt ˌwɔznt ˌveri ˌfrendli‖

Other intonation marks are the same as for the Glide-Down and Glide-Up:

‖ʃiː wəz 'kwait ᵛkaind‖ ‖ai 'mei biː 'eib‖ tə 'kʌm ɔn ᵛmʌndi‖

Also:

‖ʃiː ˌsed ʃiː wəz 'kwait ˋpliːzd əˌbaut it‖

Start practising on three syllables: fall on the first, keep the second low and rise on the third. Do it slowly and sing them if necessary:

‖ˋʃiː ˌwount ˌhelp‖ ‖ˋai ˌdount ˌnou‖ ‖ˋðæts ˌnou ˌgud‖
‖ˋðæt wəz ˌnais‖ ‖ˋdʒɔn kən ˌkʌm‖ ‖ˋðis iz ˌmain‖

Notice that when the first syllable has a short vowel there may be a jump down to the next syllable rather than a fall. Compare:

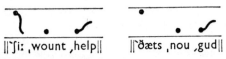

‖ˋʃiː ˌwount ˌhelp‖   ‖ˋðæts ˌnou ˌgud‖

When you are sure that you have the fall followed by the rise, speed up gradually to normal speed. Then try examples with two syllables, falling on the first (or jumping down from it) and rising on the second. Remember to start quite high:

‖ˋjuː ͵kæn‖ ‖ˋai ͵kɑːnt‖ ‖ˋdʒɔn ͵dʌz‖ ‖ˋðæts ͵nais‖ ‖ˋpæt ͵keim‖

‖ᵛtjuːzdi‖ ‖ᵛfraidi‖ ‖ᵛsʌndi‖ ‖ᵛeiprəl‖ ‖ᵛɔːgəst‖ ‖ᵛeiti‖ ‖ᵛsiksti‖

Next try the Dive on one syllable. Do it very slowly at first on three notes: high–low–high:

‖ᵛtuː‖ ‖ᵛfɔː‖ ‖ᵛnain‖ ‖ᵛmiː‖ ‖ᵛjuː‖ ‖ᵛsuːn‖ ‖ᵛpliːz‖ ‖ᵛtrai‖

Then gradually speed up and stop singing. Now try with short vowels:

‖ᵛten‖ ‖ᵛhim‖ ‖ᵛsiŋ‖ ‖ᵛkʌm‖ ‖ᵛbæd‖ ‖ᵛlɔŋ‖ ‖ᵛgud‖ ‖ᵛbɔb‖ ‖ᵛæn‖

The voicing of the final consonant will help you with those —the rising part of the Dive is on the final consonant, so use it.

More difficult are the short vowels followed by consonants with no voice, but you may lengthen the vowel a little to give you time to make both the fall and the rise:

‖ᵛsiks‖ ‖ᵛðis‖ ‖ᵛwitʃ‖ ‖ᵛðæt‖ ‖ᵛwɔt‖ ‖ᵛʌs‖ ‖ᵛstɔp‖ ‖ᵛjes‖

Always be sure that you start high, go low and finish higher. Now some longer examples, which are easier, rather like a fall followed by a Take-Off. Keep the syllables after the fall down low until you reach the rise:

‖ˋai ͵kudn̩t ͵help it‖ ‖ˋsʌmwʌnz ͵gɔt tə ͵duː it‖ ‖ˋmɛəri wud ͵prɔbəbli ͵tel juː‖ ‖ˋdʒɔn ͵keim ͵houm tə͵dei‖ ‖ˋsevrəl ͵piːpl əv ͵tould miː ðei ͵θɔːt it ͵lukt ͵priti‖

Now try adding other words before the fall-rise:

‖ˈdount ᵛwʌri‖ ‖ˈdount bi ᵛleit‖ ‖juː ˈmʌsn̩t ᵛluːz it‖ ‖juː kən ˈhæv it fər ə ˈkʌpl əv ᵛdeiz‖

THE DIVE

‖'trai 'nɔt tə ˋbreik ˏðæt‖
‖ai 'went 'ʌp tə 'lʌndən bai ˋkɑː təˏdei‖
‖'dʒɔn 'tould miː hiː wəz 'gouiŋ ɔn ˋhɔlədi ˏneks ˏwiːk‖
‖ai 'hiə ðɛəz 'biːn ə 'greit 'diːl əv ˋtrʌb‖ əˏbaut ˏðæt‖

HOW TO USE THE TUNES
Statements

1. Use the Glide-Down for statements which are *complete* and *definite*: ‖it wəz 'kwait ˋgud‖ ‖ai 'laikt it 'veri ˋmʌtʃ‖ ‖ai 'wudn̩t 'maind 'siːiŋ it əˋgen‖.

2. If the statement is intended to be *soothing* or *encouraging* use the Glide-Up: ‖ai 'ʃɑːnt bi ˏlɔŋ‖ ‖'dʒɔn ‖ bi 'hiə ˏsuːn‖ ‖ai 'wount 'draiv 'tuː ˏfɑːst‖ (so don't worry).

3. If the statement is a *grumble*, use the Take-Off: ‖ai ˏdidn̩t ˏhəːt juː‖ (so why make all that fuss?). ‖juː ˏkɑːnt ˏpɔsəbli ˏduː ˏðæt‖ (you ought to know better). ‖ai ˏdid‖ (grumbling contradiction).

4. If the statement is *not complete* but leading to a following word-group, use the Dive:

‖ai ˇlukt ət im‖ (ən 'rekəgnaizd im ət ˋwʌns‖).
‖ʃiː 'tuk ðə ˇkɑː‖ (ən 'drouv tə ˋlʌndən‖).
‖wen'evər iː 'kʌmz tə ˇvizit əs‖ (hiː 'traiz tə 'bɔrou ˋmʌni‖).

5. If the statement is intended *as a question* use the Glide-Up: ‖juː ˏlaik it?‖ ‖juː 'kɑːnt ˏgou?‖ ‖hiː 'dʌzn̩t 'wɔnt tə ˏlend juː it?‖

6. For statements which show *reservations* on the part of the speaker and which might be followed by *but*... or by *you must admit* or *I must admit* use the Dive:

‖hiːz ˇdʒenərəs‖ (but I don't trust him).
‖hiːz ˇhænsəm‖ (you must admit).
‖ai kud 'teik juː 'ðɛə təˇmɔrou‖ (but not today).
‖ai 'laik jɔː ˇhæt‖ (I must admit).
‖it 'wɔzn̩t ə 'veri 'nais 'θiŋ tə ˇduː‖ (you must admit).

7. If the statement is a *correction* of what someone else has said, use the Dive:

(He's forty-five) ‖ˈfɔːti ˇsiks‖
(I like him a lot) ‖ju: ˋjuːs tə ˌlaik im‖
(I can't do it) ‖ju: ˈkɑːnt ˈduː it ˋðæt ˌwei‖

8. If the statement is a *warning*, use the Dive: ‖ju: l bi ˇleit‖ ‖ai ˈʃɑːnt ˈtel ju: əˇgen‖ ‖ju: ˈmʌsn̩t ˋʃeik it ˌtuː ˌmʌtʃ‖

9. If the statement has two parts, of which the first is *more important* to the meaning than the second, use the Dive, with the fall at the end of the first part and the rise at the end of the second:

‖ai ˈwent tə ˋlʌndən ɔn ˌmʌndi‖
‖ju: kən ˋkiːp it if ju: ˌriəli ˌwɔnt it‖
‖hi: wəz ˈveri ˋwel wen ai ˌlɑːst ˌsɔː im‖
‖ai m ˈveri ˋkʌmfətəbl̩ ˌθæŋk ju:‖

Wh-questions (containing Which, What, Who, etc.)

10. Use the Glide-Up if you want to show as much *interest* in the other person as in the subject: ‖ˈhau z jɔː ˌdɔːtə?‖ ‖ˈwen ə ju: ˈkʌmiŋ tə ˌsiː əs?‖ ‖ˈwen did ju: get ˈbæk frəm ˌhɔlədi?‖

11. Use the Glide-Down if you want the question to sound more *business-like* and interested in the subject and also for one-word questions (unless they are repetition-questions, see 12).

‖ˈwai did ju: ˈtʃeindʒ jɔː ˋmaind?‖
‖ˈhuː ɔn ˈəːθ wəz ˋðæt?‖ ‖ˋwitʃ?‖

12. For *repetition-questions*, when you are repeating someone else's question or when you want the other person to repeat some information, use the Take-Off:

||ˌwen did ai ˑgou?|| (Or where?)
||ˌwai?|| (Because I wanted to.)
(I arrived at ten o'clock.) ||ˌwen?||
(It took me two hours.) ||ˌhau ˑlɔŋ?||
(John told me to do it.) ||ˌhuː ˑtould juː tə ˑduː it?||

Notice that in examples like the last three, where the other person is being asked to repeat information, the rise begins on the wh-word.

Yes-No questions (questions answerable by Yes or No)

13. For *short questions* used as responses, like *Did you?*, *Has she?*, etc., use the Glide-Down:

(John's on holiday.) ||ˋiz iː?||
(I went to the theatre last night.) ||ˋdid juː?||

14. For all other Yes-No questions use the Glide-Up:

	ˈhæv juː ˌsiːn im ˑjet?	
	ˈdid ˈdʒɔn ˈpoust ˈðæt ˌletə?	
	ˈkæn ai ˌsiː it?	

Notice that the Glide-Up is also used for repetition-questions of this type:

(Have you seen him yet?) ||ˈhæv ˌai ˑsiːn im ˑjet?||
(Will you help me?) ||ˈwil ai ˌhelp juː?||

Tag-questions (short Yes-No questions added on to statements or commands)

15. For tag-questions *after commands* use the Take-Off:

	ˈkʌm ouvə ˋhiə	ˌwil juː?	
	ˈlets ˈhæv səm ˋmjuːzik	ˌʃæl wiː?	
	ˈhould ˋðis fɔː miː	ˌwud juː?	

16. If both the statement and the tag question have *not* in them, or if *not* is missing from both, use the Take-Off:

‖hiː ˈhæzn̩t əˋraivd | ˏhæzn̩t iː?‖
‖juː ˋlaikt it | ˏdid juː?‖
‖ðei d ˈlaik səm ˋmɔː | ˏwud ðei?‖

17. Where the word *not* occurs in either the statement or the tag question (but not in both, see 16) use the Glide-Down to force the other person to *agree* with you:

‖its ˋkould təˌdei | ˋizn̩t it?‖   (Forcing the answer *Yes*.)
‖it wəz ə ˈveri ˈgud ˋfilm | ˋwɔzn̩t it?‖
‖juː ˏwount ˏwʌri | ˋwil juː?‖   (Forcing the answer *No*.)
‖hiː ˈkɑːnt ˈriəli ˇhelp it | ˋkæn iː?‖

18. When you don't want to force the other person to agree with you, but to *give his opinion*, use the Take-Off:

‖jɔː ˈkʌmiŋ tə ˋtiː wið əs | ˏɑːnt juː?‖
‖juː ˈwəːnt ˋhiər ɔn ˏwednz̩di | ˏwəː juː?‖
‖hiː ˏdidn̩t ˏluk ˏil | ˏdid iː?‖

Commands

19. If you want the command to sound like a *pleading request* use the Dive, with the fall on *Do* or *Don't* if they occur or on the main verb if not, and the rise at the end:

‖ˇʃʌt ðə ˏwindou‖   ‖ˋduː ˏhæv səm ˏmɔː ˏtiː‖
‖ˋsend it əz ˏsuːn əz juː ˏkæn‖   ‖ˋdount ˏmeik miː ˏæŋgri‖

Notice commands with only one important word:

‖ˇtrai‖   ‖ˇteik it‖   ‖ˇlend it tə ðəm‖

20. For *strong commands* use the Glide-Down:

‖ˈdount biː ə ˈstjuːpid ˋidiət‖   ‖ˈteik jɔː ˋfiːt ɔf ðə ˏtʃɛə‖
‖ˈkʌm ən ˈhæv ˋdinə wið əs‖   ‖ˈhæv səm ˋtʃiːz‖

Exclamations

21. For *strong exclamations* use the Glide-Down:

‖'gud ˋhevǝnz!‖   ‖'hau ikˋstrɔːdn̩ri!‖
‖wɔt ǝ 'veri 'priti ˋdres!‖   ‖ˋnɔnsǝns!‖   ‖ˋsplendid!‖

Remember that *Thank you* comes in this class when it expresses real gratitude:

‖ˋθæŋk juː‖   ‖'θæŋk juː 'veri ˋmʌtʃ‖

22. For *greetings* and for saying *goodbye* use the Glide-Up:

‖'gud ˌmɔːning‖   ‖'hʌˌlou‖   ‖'gud ˌbai‖   ‖'gud ˌnait‖

23. If the exclamation is *questioning* use the Take-Off:

‖ˌou?‖   ‖ˌriǝli?‖   ‖ˌwel?‖

24. For exclamations which refer to something *not very exciting or unexpected* use the Glide-Up:

‖ˌθæŋk juː‖   ‖ˌgud‖   ‖'ɔːl ˌrait‖   ‖'gud ˌlʌk‖

The 24 rules given here for using the tunes will help you to choose a tune which is suitable for whatever you want to say. This does not mean that English speakers always follow these rules; if you listen carefully to their intonation (as you must!) you will notice that they often use tunes which are not recommended here for a statement or command, etc. You must try to find out *what* tunes they use and *when*, and just what they mean when they do it. But if you study the rules carefully and use the tunes accordingly you will at least be using them in an English way, even though you will not have the same variety or flexibility in their use that an English speaker has. This will only come with careful, regular listening and imitation. Don't be afraid to imitate what you hear, whether it is sounds or rhythm or intonation, even though it may sound funny to you at first. It won't sound half as funny to an English ear as it does to you, and in any case you'll soon get used to it!

EXERCISES ON CHAPTER 7

(Do not look at the answers on p. 165 until you have completed all these exercises.)

1. Practise again all the examples given in this chapter. Be sure that you understand the relation between the short and the long way of showing the intonation.

2. Transcribe the following conversation phonetically; divide it into word groups and rhythm units and then underline the important words:

Can you recommend somewhere for a holiday?

What an odd coincidence! I was just going to tell you about our holiday!

Really? Where did you go? To the South of France again?

No, this time we went to Ireland!

Oh, you went to Ireland, did you? You were thinking about it the last time we met.

Oh yes, I mentioned it to you, didn't I?

You were thinking of Belfast, weren't you?

Dublin. But we didn't go there in the end.

Didn't you? Where did you go?

Where? To Galway.

That's on the West coast, isn't it? Was the weather good?

Reasonably good.

Tell me about the prices there, would you?

They weren't too bad. You should go there and try it. But you ought to go soon. Summer's nearly over!

It isn't over yet. But thank you very much for your advice.

Good luck. Have a good time.

Thank you. Goodbye.

3. Study the rules for using the tunes and then re-arrange them so that all the rules concerning the Glide-Down are brought together; and similarly with those concerning the Glide-Up, the Take-Off and the Dive.

4. Using the rules, mark the intonation of each word group in the conversation in 2. After you have finished the whole conversation check your marking carefully with the answer on p. 166 and notice any differences. Then practise saying each part of it separately until you are satisfied that it is correct, and finally put the parts together so that you can say the whole thing fluently, rhythmically, and with English sounds and intonation.

CONVERSATIONAL PASSAGES FOR PRACTICE

||ˋðæts əˌnais ˏsjuːt || ai'hævn̩t ˋsiːnit biˏfɔː | ˏhævai||

||ˋnou | itsðə'fəːs 'taim aivˋwɔːnit ˏæktʃəli || ai'ounli ˋgɔtit əˌbaut ˌfɔː ˌdeiz əˏgou || juːˋlaikit | ˏduːjuː ||

||'veri ˋmʌtʃ || 'didjuː 'hævit 'speʃli ˏmeid | ɔː'didjuː 'baiit 'ɔf ðəˋpeg||

||ai 'hædit ˋmeid || ai'veri ˋrɛəli ˌbai əˏsjuːt | souai'θɔːt aid 'hævit ˋteiləd | ənaim'kwait ˋpliːzdwiðit||

||aiʃudˋθiŋksou || its'veri ˋhænsəm || 'meiai 'ɑːsk 'wɛə juːˏgɔtit||

||ðə'seim 'pleis əzai'gɔt maiˋlɑːstwʌn | 'naintiːn ˋjiəz əˌgou||

||'naintiːn ˏjiəz || dəjuː'riəli 'miːn tə'telmiː juː'hævn̩t 'hæd ə'sjuːt sinsˏðen||

||'ðæts ˏrait || ai'dount 'ɔfn̩ ˋwɛər əˌsjuːt juːˌsiː | souðei'tend tə'lɑːst ə'lɔŋ ˋtaim||

||'naintiːn 'jiəz iz'səːtn̩li ə'lɔŋ ˇtaim || ən'iːvən ifjuː'dount ˋwɛəðəm ˌmʌtʃ | jɔːr'ouldwʌn 'mʌstəv 'lɑːstid ˇwel||

||ˋou | itˋdid || ðei ˌdid ə'veri 'gud ˋdʒɔbɔnit||

||ˏwɔt wəzðə·neim əvðə·teilə||

||ˋfilipsn̩ || its'kwait əˋsmɔːl ˏʃɔp | 'rait ətðiː'end əvˋkiŋ ˌstriːt||

||'ai ˏnouit || 'rɑːðər əˋʃæbi ˌlukiŋ ˌpleis || aiv'nevəbiːn ˇinðɛə||

||ai'wudn̩t 'kɔːlit ˇʃæbi | bətit'izn̩t 'veri ˇmɔdn̩ | aiədˋmit || hauˋevə | ðeiə'veri əˋblaidʒiŋ | ən ˌteik ə'greit 'diːl əvˋtrʌbl̩||

||'sou aikənˋsiː || ai'θiŋk ail'gou əˋlɔŋðɛə || aiˋniːd əˌnjuː ˏsjuːt || ˋou | 'bai ðəˋwei | 'wɔt 'sɔːt əvˋpraisiz dəðeiˌtʃɑːdʒ||

||'priti ˋriːznəbl̩ ˏriəli || 'ðis wəz'θəːti 'faiv ˋpaundz||

||ˋðæts ˌnɔt ˏbæd | ai'θiŋk ail'luk 'inðɛə təˋmɔrou||

||ˋjes | ˋduː || 'menʃən 'mai ˋneim ifjuːˏlaik | it'wount

'duːeni ˇhɑːm | ənit'mait 'duː səm◟gud ‖ aiv'dʒʌs 'peid mai◟bil‖

‖ai'niːd ə'kʌp| əv◟ʃəːts | 'grei ◟terəliːn ˌpliːz‖

‖◟səːtn̩li ˌsəː | ail'dʒʌs 'getsʌm ◟aut ‖ 'wudjuː 'maind 'teikiŋ əˌsiːt fərə·moumənt ‖ ai'ʃɑːnt biˌlɔŋ‖

‖◟nou | ◟dount biˌtuː ˌlɔŋ | ai'hævn̩t 'veri 'mʌtʃ ◟taim‖

‖'veri ˌgud ˌsəː ‖ ◟hiəz əˌnais ˌʃəːt | wiː'sel ə◟lɔt əvˌðiswʌn‖

‖◟duːjuː ˌnau ‖ ◟jes | itsðə'sɔːtəv ◟stail aiˌwɔnt | bətai'ɑːst fə◟grei ‖ 'ðisiz ◟pəːp|‖

‖ˌpəːp| ·səː | ◟ʃuəli ˌnɔt ‖ its'wɔt 'wiː 'kɔːl 'silvə ◟bluː‖

‖welit'luks ◟pəːp| təˌmiː ‖ ◟eniwei | aid'laik 'sʌmθiŋ ə'lit| 'les ◟brait ‖ 'mɔː 'laik ðə'wʌn aim◟wɛəriŋ‖

‖◟ou | ◟ðæt ˌsɔːt əvˌgrei | ai'hævn̩t 'siːn 'ðæt fə◟jiəz‖

‖ai'bɔːtit 'hiə 'siks ◟mʌnθs əˌgou‖

‖'didjuː ˌriəli ·səː ‖ it'mʌstəvbiːn 'ould ◟stɔk‖

‖wel'siː ifjuː'stil gɔt'eni ◟left | ˌwiljuː‖

‖◟ɑː ˌjes | ◟hiə wiːˌɑː ‖ aim◟sɔri əˌbaut ðəˌdʌst ·səː ‖ 'kænai 'lendjuː əˌhæŋkətʃiːf|‖

‖'nou ˌθæŋkjuː | 'ail səˌvaiv ‖ ◟jes | ◟ðæt ˌluks ˌbetə ‖ 'hævjuː əˌnʌðəwʌn ·laikit‖

‖aimə'freid ◟nɔt ˌsəː | its'prɔbəbli ðə'lɑːst inðə◟kʌntri‖

‖◟ou | ◟ɔːlˌrait | ail◟teikit ‖ 'haumʌtʃ ◟izit‖

‖'fɔː ◟giniz ˌsəː | itwəzə'veri 'gud ◟ʃəːt initsˌtaim ‖

‖aiʃud◟θiŋk ˌsou ətˌfɔː ˌginiz ‖ 'kænai 'pei baiˌtʃek‖

‖◟səːtn̩li ˌsəː | 'wudjuː 'dʒʌs 'putjɔː 'neim ənə'dres ɔnðəˌbæk‖

‖aikən'nevər ʌndə◟stænd ˌðæt ‖ 'if ðə'tʃek wəz'nou ˇgud | aid'put ə◟fɔls ˌneim ənəˌdres | 'wudn̩t ˌjuː‖

‖jɔː◟dʒoukiŋ ˌsəːr | əv◟kɔːs ‖ ai'nætʃərəli ə'sjuːm jɔː'tʃek iz◟gud‖

‖'veri ◟trʌstiŋ ˌɔvjuː ‖ it◟iz əzəˌmætər əvˌfækt‖

‖izðɛər'eniθiŋ ˌels juːˈniːd ·səː ‖ ˌtaiz | ˌsɔks | ˌstʌdz‖

‖aiˌdount ˌθiŋk ·sou | ˌθæŋkjuː ‖ 'gud ˌmɔːniŋ‖

‖'gud ˌdei ·səː‖

‖ˋjɔːr əˌgɑːdn̩ər ǀ ˋɑːntjuː ‖ dəˈjuːnou ˈeniθiŋ əˈbaut ˈbizi ˌliziz‖

‖əˈbaut ˌwɔt ǀ ˈbizi ˌliziz ‖ wɔtənˈəːθ əˋðei‖

‖ˋou ǀ aiˈθɔːtjuːd ˋnou ǀ ðeiəˋhaus ˌplɑːnts ‖ aivˈdʒʌsbiːn ˋgivn̩wʌn ǀ baimaiˋsistər ǀ ənaiˈwɔnt təˈnou ˈhau təluk-ˋɑːftərit‖

‖aiməˈfreid aiˈdount ˋnou ˌmʌtʃ əˌbaut ˌhaus ·plɑːnts ‖ bətaivˈgɔt əˋbuk ˌsʌmwɛə ðətˌmait ˌhelp ‖ ˈlets ˋsiː ‖ ˋɑː ˌjes ǀ ˋhiər itˌiz‖

‖ðəˋkɛər əvˋhaus ˌplɑːnts ‖ ˋmː ǀ ˋðæt ˌluks ˌjuːsfḷ‖

‖dəjuːˈhæpən təˈnou ðə ˌlætin ·neiməvit‖

‖aiməˈfreid aiˋdount ‖ ˈbizi ˋliziz ðiːˌounli ˌneim ˌaiv ·həːd‖

‖ˈwɔt dəzitˋluk ˌlaik‖

‖welitsˌgɔt əˈrɑːðə ˈwɔːtəri ˈlukiŋ ˇstem ǀ ˈveri ˈpeil ˌgriːn ǀ ənˈfɛəli ˈsmɔːl ˈpiŋk ˋflauəz‖

‖ˈhau ˈmeni ˋpetǀz‖

‖ˈgud ˋgreiʃəs ǀ aivˈnevə ˋkauntidðəm ‖ ˈfɔːr ɔːˋfaiv aisə-ˌpouz ‖ ðeiəˈrɑːðə ˈlaik ˈwaild ˋrouz ˌpetǀz‖

‖ailˈlukʌp ˈbizi ˈlizi inðiːˋindeks ‖ ðeiˋmei ˌgivit ‖ ˋjes ǀ ˋhiər itˌiz ǀ ˌpeidʒ ˈnainti ˋeit ‖ ˋðɛər ǀ ˈiz ˌðætit‖

‖ˈmai ˋwəːd ǀ ˋðæts əˌbigwʌn ‖ ˈmainz ˈounli ˈgɔt ˋwʌn ˌstem ǀ ənˈðæt ˈsiːmz təˈhæv ˋdʌzn̩z ǀ bətaiˈθiŋk itsðəˈseim ˇwʌn‖

‖welðeiˈlaik ˇlait ǀ bətˈnɔt ˋhiːt ‖ ˈwɔːtəðəm ˈwel inðəˇsʌmə ǀ bətˈnɔt ˈveri ˈmʌtʃ inˋwintə ‖ ənˈðæts əˈbaut ˋɔːl ‖ ˋou ǀ ˋðæts ˌrɑːðə ˌnais ǀ itˈsez ˇhiə ǀ ðətðəˋdʒəːmən ˌneimfərit ǀ ˌmiːnz inˈdʌstriəs iˋlizəbəθ ‖ ˈmʌtʃ ˈgrændə ðənˈbizi ˇlizi‖

‖aiˈθiŋk aidˈrɑːðə hævəˈbizi ˋlizi inmaiˌhaus ǀ ðənənin-ˈdʌstriəs iˋlizəbəθ ‖ bətˈθæŋkjuː ˈveri ˋmʌtʃ ǀ aimˈveri ˋgreitfḷ ˌtuːjuː ‖ ˈpræps ailbiːˈeibḷ təˈkiːpit əˋlaiv ˌnau ǀ aiˈjuːʒuəli ˈhæv ədiˋzɑːstrəs iˌfekt ɔnˌplɑːnts‖

‖aiʃudˈounli ˈwɔːtərit ˈwʌns əˋmʌnθ ˌnau ǀ ʌnˈtil ðəˋspriŋ ‖ ˋʌðə ˌwaiz ǀ juːlˈprɔbəbli ˋkilit‖

‖ˋgud ǀ ailˋduː ˌðæt ‖ ˈθæŋks əˋgen‖

ANSWERS TO EXERCISES

CHAPTER 1 (p. 16)

1. *write*, 3 /r, ai, t/; *through*, 3 /θ, r, u:/; *measure*, 4 /m, e, ʒ, ə/; *six*, 4 /s, i, k, s/; *half*, 3 /h, ɑ:, f/; *where*, 2 /w, ɛə/; *one*, 3 /w, ʌ, n/; *first*, 4 /f, ə:, s, t/; *voice*, 3 /v, ɔi, s/; *castle*, 4 /k, ɑ:, s, l/; *scissors*, 5 /s, i, z, ə, z/; *should*, 3 /ʃ, u, d/; *judge*, 3 /dʒ, ʌ, dʒ/; *father*, 4 /f, ɑ:, ð, ə/; *lamb*, 3 /l, æ, m/.

2. Some examples are: *for, four, fore* fɔ:; *see, sea* si:; *sent, scent, cent* sent; *sole, soul* soul; *choose, chews* tʃu:z; *herd, heard* hə:d; *meet, meat, mete* mi:t; *too, to, two* tu:; *sight, site* sait.

3. rait, θru:, meʒə, siks, hɑ:f, wɛə, wʌn, fə:st, vɔis, kɑ:sl, sizəz, ʃud, dʒʌdʒ, fɑ:ðə, læm.

mæt, met, mi:t, meit, mait, kɔt, kʌt, kɔ:t, lik, luk, bə:d, bɔ:d, loud, laud, bɔiz, bɑ:z, bɛəz, ʃiə, ʃuə, kɔpə, gri:n, tʃɑ:dʒ, sɔŋ, faiv, wið, tru:θ, jelou, pleʒə, həlou.

4. mʌðə, fɑ:ðə separate /m, ʌ, f, ɑ:/.

CHAPTER 2 (p. 30)

2. Complete obstruction (glottal stop); vibration (voice); and open position (breath).

4. You cannot sing a voiceless sound; tune depends on variations in the frequency of vibrations of the vocal cords, and voiceless sounds have no vibrations.

5. It allows the breath stream to pass into the nasal cavity, or prevents it.

10. The tongue moves from a low to a high front position for ai, from a low back to a high front position for ɔi, and from a low to a high back position for au.

12. The side teeth gently bite the sides of the tongue because the sides are touching the sides of the palate and the side teeth.

CHAPTER 3 (p. 82)

1. You should concentrate on the phoneme difficulties first.

CHAPTER 5 (p. 112)

4. bæg, bæk; kʌb, kʌp; hɑːv, hɑːf; lɔg, lɔk; kɔːd, kɔːt; puɫ, puʃ; luːz, luːs; səːdʒ, səːtʃ; seiv, seif; raiz, rais; dʒɔiz, dʒɔis (*Joyce*); koud, kout; hauz (vb.), haus (n.); fiəz, fiəs; skɛəz, skɛəs; buəz (*boors*), buəs (*Bourse*).

CHAPTER 6 (p. 133)

1, 6, 8. ‖aiv*niːdid səm*nju: *buk *ʃelvz | fərə*lɔŋ *taim ‖ sou*djuəriŋ mai*hɔlədi | aidi*saidid tə*tækǀ ðə*dʒɔb mai-*self ‖ *nɔt ðətaim*veri *klevə wiðmai*hændz | bətit*didn̩t *siːm *tuː *difikǀt | ənəzaidɔːl*redi *sed ðətwiː*kudn̩t ə*fɔːd tə*gou ə*wei | ai*θɔːt itədbi*pruːdn̩t | *nɔt tə*spend *mʌni | *hæviŋit *dʌn prə*feʃənəli ‖ ai*bɔːt ðə*wud | ətðə*loukǀ *hændi *krɑːft *ʃɔp ‖ ənaihæd*plenti əv*skruːz ‖ bətai*faund ðətmai*ould *sɔː | witʃədbiːn*left bi*haind baiðə*priːviəs *ounər əvðə*haus | *wɔzn̩t *gud i*nʌf ‖ ənaidi*saidid tə*bai ə*njuːwʌn ‖ *ðæt wəzmai*fəːst mi*steik ‖ mai*sekənd | wəztə*gou təðə*bigist *aiən *mʌŋgər in*lʌndən | ən*ɑːsk fərə*sɔː ‖ juːd*θiŋk itwəz*simpǀ | *wudn̩tju: | tə*bai ə*sɔː | bətit*izn̩t ‖ ai*sed təðə*mæn bi*haind ðə*kauntə | ai*wɔnt ə*sɔː ‖ hiːwəzə*nais *mæn | ən*didiz *best fə*miː ‖ *jessə | *wɔt *kaind əv*sɔː ‖ *ou | ə*sɔː fə*kʌtiŋ *wud ‖ *jessə | bətwiːhæv*fif *tiːn *difrənt *kaindz | fə*difrənt *dʒɔbz ‖ *wɔt didju:*wɔntit *fɔː ‖ aiik*spleind ə*baut mai*buk *ʃelvz | ən*felt laikən*ignərənt *fuːl inə*wəːld əv*ekspəːts ‖ witʃ-wəz*truː ‖ hiː*sɔː ðətaiwəzə*nɔvis | ənwəz*veri *kaind ‖ hiː*touldmi: *wɔt aiʃud*niːd | ənəd*vaizdmi: tə*hæv ə*leidiz *saiz ‖ *iːziə tə*mænidʒ fəðəbi*ginəsə: ‖ hiː*wɔzn̩t *biːiŋ *nɑːsti | *dʒʌst *helpful ‖ ənaiwəz*greitful *tuːim ‖ hiː*ɔːlsou

*souldmiː | ə*buk ɔn*wudwəːk fə*skuːl *bɔiz ‖ ənaivbiːn-
*riːdiŋit wið*greit *intrəst ‖ ðə*neksttaim aimɔn*hɔlədi |
aiʃ|*meik ə*staːt ɔnðə*ʃelvz‖.

2. ‖ðei *keim tə ðə *dɔː‖. ‖ðɛə wə *tuː əv ðəm‖.
‖*wɔt ə juː sə*praizd æt‖. ‖ʃiː z əz *ould əz ðə *hilz‖.
‖ʃiː hæz ən *ʌŋk| ən ə *kʌzŋ‖. ‖ai ʃ| biː *æŋgri|‖.
‖*huːl *miːt im ət ðiː *ɛə *pɔːt‖. ‖*ai *wil‖.
‖*wɔts əː *foun *nʌmbə‖. ‖*wɔt dəz *ðæt *mætə‖.
‖ai d *laik səm *tiː‖. ‖wel *meik *sʌm‖.
‖*wɔts *dʒɔn *kʌm fɔː‖. ‖fər iz *sɔː ðət juː *bɔroud‖.
‖*wɔt kən ai *duː‖. ‖*mɔː ðən *ai *kæn‖.
‖hiː wəz *pliːzd *wɔzŋt iː‖. ‖əv *kɔːs iː *wɔz‖.
‖*wen əm ai *gouiŋ tə *get it‖. ‖ai m *nɔt *ʃuə‖.
‖ai v *teikən it frəm ðə *ʃelf‖. ‖*jes ai *θɔːt juː *hæd‖.
‖ðei d ɔːl*redi *red it‖. ‖bət *sou əd *ai‖.

3. Have, some, for, a. To, the. That, am, but, not, and,
as, had, that, not, to, would, be, to. The, at, the, and, of,
but, that, had, the, of, the, not, and, to, a. Was. Was, to,
to, the, and, for, a. Would, was, to, a. But, not. To, the,
the, a. Was, a, and, his. Of. A, for. But, for. And, an, a, of,
was. That, was, a, and, was. And, to, a. To, for, the. Not,
and, was, him. A, for, and, have. The, am, shall, a, the.

7. hæn(d)z, itəbbi pruːdn̩t, spen(d) ðə mʌni, dʌm prə-
feʃənəli, hændikraːf(t) ʃɔp, ai hæb plenti, ai faun(d) ðət,
oul(d) sɔː, witʃ əb biːn, lef(t) bihain(d) bai, wɔzŋ̍k gud,
fəːs(t) misteik, wudn̩tʃuː, bihain(d) ðə kauntə, bes(t) fə miː,
wɔk kaind, difrəŋk kaindz, toul(d) miː, ədvaiz(d) miː, wɔzm̩p
biːiŋ, helpf|, greitf|, soul(d) miː, neks(t) taim.

CHAPTER 7 (p. 158)

2, 4. The number in brackets after each word group is
the number of the rule which has been used to select an
appropriate tune.

‖'kænjuː rekə'mend 'sʌmwɛə fərə‚hɔlədi (14)‖

‖wɔtən'ɔd kouˑinsidəns (21) ‖ aiwəz'dʒʌs 'gouiŋ tə'teljuː ə'baut ˑauə ‚hɔlədi (1)‖

‖‚riəli (23) ‖ 'wɛə didjuː‚gou (10) | ðə'sauθ əv‚frɑːns ə·gen (5)‖

‖ˑnou (1) | ˑðis ‚taim (4) | wiː'went tuːˑaiələnd (1)‖

‖ˑou (21) | juː'went tuːˑaiələnd (1) | ‚didjuː (16) ‖ juːwə-ˑθiŋkiŋ ə‚bautit (4) | ðəˑlɑːs ‚taim wiː‚met (1)‖

‖'ou ˑjes (1) | aiˑmenʃəndit ‚tuːjuː (1) | ˑdidn̩tai (17)‖

‖juːwə'θiŋkiŋ əvbelˑfɑːst (1) | ‚wəːntjuː (18)‖

‖ˑdʌblin (7) | bətwiː'didn̩t ˑgouðɛər inðiː‚end (9)‖

‖ˑdidn̩tjuː (13) ‖ 'wɛə ˑdidjuː ‚gou (11)‖

‖‚wɛə (12) ‖ təˑgɔlwei (1)‖

‖'ðæts ɔnðə'west ˑkoust (1) | ‚izn̩tit (18) ‖ 'wɔz ðə ‚weðə ·gud (14)‖

‖ˑriːznəbli ‚gud (6)‖

‖'telmiː ə'baut ðəˑpraisiz ‚ðɛə (20) | ‚wudjuː (15)‖

‖ðei'wəːnt 'tuː ‚bæd (2) ‖ juːʃudˑgou ‚ðɛə (1) | ən'traiit (1)‖ bətjuː'ɔːt tə'gou ˑsuːn (8) | 'sʌməz 'niəli ˑouvə (1)‖

‖it‚izn̩t ‚ouvə ‚jet (3) | bət'θæŋkjuː ˑveri 'mʌtʃ fəjɔːrədˑvais (21)‖

‖'gud ‚lʌk (24) ‖ ˑhævə ‚gud ‚taim (19)‖

‖ˑθæŋkjuː (21) ‖ 'gud‚bai (22)‖

3. *Glide-Down:* Rules 1, 11, 13, 17, 20, 21.
   Glide-Up: Rules 2, 5, 10, 14, 22, 24.
   Take-Off: Rules 3, 12, 15, 16, 18, 23.
   Dive: Rules 4, 6, 7, 8, 9, 19.

APPENDIX 1

THE DIFFICULTIES OF ENGLISH PRONUNCIATION FOR SPEAKERS OF ARABIC, CANTONESE, FRENCH, GERMAN, HINDI AND SPANISH

On the following pages are very short summaries of the main difficulties in English pronunciation for speakers of six major languages (Arabic, Cantonese, French, German, Hindi and Spanish). Some of the consonants and vowels are referred to as equivalent in English and the other language, but you must understand that this does not mean that you need not bother with these sounds. It means that these sounds are independent in the language concerned, that they are a useful starting-point for acquiring the correct English sound and that they will probably not cause any misunderstanding if they are used in English.

In some cases an equivalent sound may be very different from the English one, e.g. the tongue-tip trill for /r/ in Arabic and Spanish, but English listeners will nevertheless recognize it as /r/. Sometimes, also, the equivalent of the English sound is not the one which first comes to mind (or which is most often used by the learner), but it is there and can be found. An example is /ʌ/ for French speakers: they usually use a vowel which is quite foreign to English (the vowel in Fr. *œuf* 'egg') when the vowel in Fr. *patte* 'paw' would be very much nearer.

The main difficulties are listed and speakers of these languages are advised to pay special attention to those parts of this book which deal with these difficulties, but do not assume that these are the only difficulties; for everyone, including the many readers whose languages are not discussed here, the only reliable guide is a critical ear and, if possible, a good teacher.

ARABIC (CAIRO COLLOQUIAL)
Consonants

Equivalents. /f, s, z, ʃ, h, t, k, b, d, g, tʃ, m, n, l, j, w, r/.

Difficulties. 1. /f/ and /v/ may be confused, /f/ being used for both, but /v/ may occur in Arabic in borrowed names.

2. /θ/ and /ð/ do not occur in Arabic and are replaced by /s/ and /z/.

3. /ʒ/ occurs in Arabic only in borrowed words and is often replaced by either /ʃ/ or /z/.

4. /p/ and /b/ are confused, /b/ being used for both.

5. /t/ and /d/ are dental stops in Arabic.

6. Stops are not generally exploded in final position in Arabic and the strong stops are often unaspirated.

7. /tʃ/ and /dʒ/ may be confused, /tʃ/ being used for both, though in practice /dʒ/ does not usually give difficulty.

8. /ŋ/ does not occur independently in Arabic and is replaced by /ŋk/ or /ŋg/.

9. /r/ is a tongue-tip trill in Arabic and is often used before consonants and before a pause.

10. /l/ occurs in both its clear and dark forms in Arabic, but they are distributed differently and may sometimes be interchanged in English.

Sequences of three or more consonants do not occur in Arabic and careful attention must be paid to these, especially in order to prevent the occurrence of a vowel to break up the consonant sequence.

Vowels

Equivalents. /iː, e, æ, ɑː, ɔː, u, uː, ə, ai, au, ɔi/.

Difficulties. 1. /i/ and /e/ are confused, /e/ being used for both.

2. /æ/ and /ɑː/ are not entirely independent in Arabic and there is danger of replacing one by the other in some places.

3. /ʌ/ and /ɔ/ are confused, an intermediate vowel being used for both.

4. /ɑː/ is not always made long, and is then confused with /ʌ/ or /ɔ/.

5. /əː/ is replaced by a vowel of the /ʌ/ or /e/ type followed by Arabic /r/.

6. /ei/ is replaced by the usually non-diphthongal vowel in Arabic beːt 'house'.

7. /ou/ is replaced by the non-diphthongal vowel in Arabic moːz 'bananas', and this may cause confusion with English /ɔː/.

8. /iə, ɛə, uə/ are replaced by the nearest vowel sound /iː, eː, uː/ + Arabic /r/.

CANTONESE

Consonants

Equivalents. /f, s, h, p, t, k, b, d, g, tʃ, m, n, ŋ, j, w/.

Difficulties. 1. /f/ and /v/ are confused, particularly in final position where /f/ is used for both; in initial position /w/ and /v/ are confused, /w/ being used for both.

2. /θ/ and /ð/ do not occur in Cantonese and are replaced either by /t/ and /d/ or by /f/.

3. /s/ and /z/ are confused, /s/ being used for both.

4. /s/, /ʃ/ and /ʒ/ are confused, /s/ being used for all three.

5. /b, d, g/ do not occur finally in Cantonese and are confused with /p, t, k/.

6. /p, t, k/ are not exploded in final position.

7. /tʃ/ and /dʒ/ are confused, /tʃ/ being used for both.

8. /l/, /n/ and /r/ are confused in some or all positions, /l/ (often nasalized) being used for all three. Before consonants and finally /l/ is replaced by /u/.

The only consonants which occur finally in Cantonese are /p, t, k, m, n, ŋ/; the English final consonants and the differences among them need great care. Consonant sequences do not occur in Cantonese, and the English sequences, particularly the final ones, also require a great deal of practice.

Vowels

Equivalents. /iː, ʌ, ɑː, uː, əː, ə, ei, ou, ai, au, ɔi, iə, ɛə, uə/.

Difficulties. 1. /iː/ and /i/ are confused; sometimes /iː/ is used for both and sometimes /i/, depending on what follows.

2. /e/ and /æ/ are confused, an intermediate vowel being used for both; the same vowel also replaces /ei/ before consonants.

3. /ɔ/ and /ɔː/ are confused, an intermediate vowel being used for both.

4. /uː/ and /u/ are confused; sometimes /uː/ is used for both and sometimes /u/ depending on what follows.

5. /əː/ and /ə/ usually have lip-rounding. /ə/ is often replaced by other vowels because of the spelling.

6. The difference between long and short vowels and the variations of vowel length caused by the following consonant and by rhythm grouping are very difficult and need special care.

Cantonese is a tone language in which each syllable has a fixed pitch pattern. On the whole this does not make

English intonation more difficult than it is for speakers of other languages, but it does affect the rhythm and particular attention should be paid to this.

FRENCH
Consonants

Equivalents. /f, v, s, z, ʃ, ʒ, p, t, k, b, d, g, l, m, n, j, w, r/. /tʃ/ and /dʒ/, although they have no equivalents in normal French words, do not cause difficulty.

Difficulties. 1. /θ/ and /ð/ do not occur in French and are replaced by /s/ and /z/, or less commonly by /f/ and /v/.

2. /h/ does not occur in French and is omitted in English.

3. /p, t, k/ are generally not aspirated in French, which may lead to confusion with /b, d, g/ in English.

4. /t/ and /d/ are dental stops in French.

5. /ŋ/ does not occur in French and is replaced in English by the consonant at the end of French *gagne* 'earns'.

6. /l/ in French is always clear.

7. /r/ in French is usually a weak, voiced, uvular friction or glide sound.

Although sequences of four final consonants do not occur in French and sequences of three are rare, English consonant sequences cause little difficulty except when /θ, ð, h, ŋ/ are concerned.

Vowels

Equivalents. /iː, e, ʌ, ɑː, ɔ, uː, ə, ai, au/. /ɔi/ has no obvious equivalent in French but causes no difficulty.

Difficulties. 1. /iː/ and /i/ are confused, /iː/ being used for both.

2. /æ/ and /ʌ/ are confused, /ʌ/ being used for both.

3. /ɔ/ is often pronounced in a way that makes it sound like English /ʌ/.

4. /ɔ:/ is replaced by the vowel + /r/ in French *forme* 'shape', when there is a letter *r* in the spelling, or by the vowel in French *beau* 'beautiful', when there is no *r*.

5. /ou/ is replaced by the non-diphthongal vowel in French *beau*, which causes confusion with /ɔ:/.

6. /u:/ and /u/ are confused, /u:/ being used for both.

7. /ə:/ is replaced by the lip-rounded vowel + /r/ in French *heure* 'hour'.

8. /ei/ is replaced by the non-diphthongal vowel in French *gai* 'gay'.

9. /iə, ɛə, uə/ are replaced by the vowel + /r/ in French *lire* 'read', *terre* 'earth', *lourd* 'heavy'.

10. /ə/ is often replaced by other vowels because of the spelling.

Vowels are usually short in French, compared with English, and care must be taken to make the long vowels of English long enough.

Each syllable in French has approximately the same length and the same stress. English rhythm based on the stressed syllable and the resulting variations of syllable length cause great difficulty and must be given special attention, together with weak forms of words, which do not exist in French.

GERMAN

Consonants

Equivalents. /f, v, s, z, ʃ, ʒ, h, p, t, k, b, d, g, tʃ, dʒ, m, n, ŋ, l, j, r/.

Difficulties. 1. /θ/ and /ð/ do not occur in German and are replaced by /s/ and /z/.

2. /b, d, g, dʒ, v, z, ʒ/ do not occur in final position in

German, but the corresponding strong consonants /p, t, k, tʃ, f, s, ʃ/ do, which causes confusion between the two sets in English, the strong consonants being used for both.

3. /ʒ/ and /dʒ/ occur only in borrowed words in German and they may be replaced by /ʃ/ and /tʃ/.

4. The sequence /ŋg/ does not occur in German and is replaced in English by simple /ŋ/.

5. /l/ in German is always clear.

6. /w/ and /v/ are confused, /v/ being used for both.

7. /r/ in German is either a weak, voiced, uvular friction sound or a tongue-tip trill.

English consonant sequences cause no difficulty except when /θ, ð, w/ are concerned or when /b, d, g, dʒ, v, z, ʒ/ are part of a final sequence.

Vowels

Equivalents. /iː, i, e, ʌ, ɑː, ɔ, u, uː, ə, ai, au, ɔi/.

Difficulties. 1. /e/ and /æ/ are confused, /e/ being used for both.

2. /ɔː/ is replaced by the vowel + /r/ of German *Dorf* 'town' when there is a letter *r* in the spelling, or by the vowel of German *Sohn* 'son' when there is no *r*.

3. /ou/ is replaced by the non-diphthongal vowel of German *Sohn*, which causes confusion between /ɔː/ and /ou/.

4. /əː/ is replaced by the lip-rounded vowel + /r/ of German *Dörfer* 'towns'.

5. Non-final /ə/ is usually too like English /i/, and final /ə/ usually too like English /ɔ/.

6. /ei/ is replaced by the non-diphthongal vowel in German *See* 'lake'.

7. /iə, ɛə, uə/ are replaced by the vowel + /r/ of German *vier* 'four', *Herr* 'gentleman', and *Uhr* 'clock'.

German has long and short vowels as in English, but the

influence of following consonants is not so great and care must be taken in particular to shorten the long vowels when they are followed by strong consonants.

A stressed vowel at the beginning of a word and sometimes within a word is preceded by a glottal stop. This must be avoided in English for the sake of smoothness.

HINDI

Consonants

Equivalents. /s, z, ʃ, h, p, t, k, b, d, g, tʃ, dʒ, m, n, l, j, r/.

Difficulties. 1. /f/ and /p/ are confused, /p/ being used for both.

2. /θ/ and /ð/ are replaced by dental stops, which causes confusion with /t/ and /d/.

3. /z/ is sometimes replaced by /dʒ/ or /dz/.

4. /ʒ/ and /z/ are confused, /z/ (or sometimes /dʒ/ or /dz/) being used for both.

5. /t/ and /d/ are made with the extreme edge of the tongue-tip curled back to a point just behind the alveolar ridge. These *retroflex* sounds colour the whole speech and should be avoided.

6. /p, t, k/ are often made with no aspiration even though the aspirated consonants occur in Hindi; this may cause confusion with /b, d, g/.

7. /ŋ/ may occur in final position, but between vowels it is always replaced by /ŋk/ or /ŋg/.

8. /l/ is always clear in Hindi.

9. /w/ and /v/ are confused, an intermediate sound being used for both.

10. /r/ is often like the English sound in initial position, but elsewhere is a tongue-tip trill or tap.

11. Final consonants are often followed by /ə/ when they should not be, causing confusion between e.g. *bit* and *bitter*.

Vowels

Equivalents. /iː, i, æ, ʌ, ɑː, ɔ, u, uː, ə, ai, au/. /ɔi/ has no obvious equivalent in Hindi but causes no difficulty.

Difficulties. 1. /e/ is replaced by either /æ/ or /ei/.

2. /ɔ/ and /ɔː/ are confused, an intermediate sound being used for both.

3. /əː/ is replaced by /ʌ/ + Hindi /r/.

4. /ə/ in final position is often a shortened form of /ɑː/, and in all positions may be replaced by other vowels because of the spelling.

5. /ei/ is replaced by the non-diphthongal vowel in Hindi **rel** 'train', and as this vowel is often quite short it may be confused with English /i/.

6. /ou/ is replaced by the non-diphthongal vowel in Hindi **log** 'people'.

7. /iə, ɛə, uə/ are replaced by /iːʌr, eʌr, uːʌr/.

The English long vowels are made much too short by Hindi speakers, especially in final position, and care must be taken to lengthen them considerably whenever they are fully long in English.

Rhythm in Hindi is more like that of French than English. There is much less variation of length and stress and no grouping of syllables into rhythm units as in English. The wrong syllable of a word is often stressed and great care must be taken with this and with rhythm in general. There is also difficulty in identifying the important words on which tune shape partly depends.

SPANISH

Consonants

Equivalents. /f, θ, s, p, t, k, g, tʃ, m, n, l, j, w, r/.

Difficulties. 1. /v/ and /b/ are confused; sometimes /b/ replaces /v/ and sometimes the reverse. /b/ must be a complete stop in all positions, and /v/ a lip-teeth friction sound.

2. /ð/ and /d/ are confused; sometimes /d/ (a very dental variety) replaces /ð/ and sometimes the reverse. /d/ must be a complete alveolar stop in all positions, and /ð/ a dental friction sound.

3. /g/ is often replaced by a similar friction sound; this does not generally lead to misunderstanding but should be avoided; /g/ must be a complete stop in all positions.

4. /s/ and /z/ are confused, /s/ usually being used for both, though only /z/ occurs before voiced consonants. /s/ before other consonants is very weak.

5. /ʃ/ and /ʒ/ do not occur in Spanish and are both replaced by /s/.

6. /dʒ/ and /tʃ/ are confused, /tʃ/ being used for both.

7. /h/ is replaced by a strong voiceless friction sound made between the back of the tongue and the soft palate. This does not cause confusion, but gives a disagreeable effect, and the mouth friction must be avoided.

8. /t/ is very dental in Spanish.

9. /ŋ/ does not occur independently in Spanish and is replaced by /n/ or /ŋg/.

10. /l/ is always clear in Spanish.

11. /r/ in Spanish is a tongue-tip trill.

12. /p, t, k/ are not aspirated in Spanish.

The only consonant sequences which occur in Spanish are initial stop or /f/ + /r/ or /l/. Other initial sequences and practically all final sequences are very difficult and need much practice.

Vowels

Equivalents. /iː, e, ʌ, ɔ, uː, ei, ai, au, ɔi/.

Difficulties. 1. /iː/ and /i/ are confused, the replacement being a vowel usually more like /iː/ than /i/.

2. /æ/, /ʌ/ and /ɑː/ (if there is no letter *r* in the spelling) are all confused, /ʌ/ being used for all three. Where *r* occurs in the spelling, /ɑː/ is replaced by the vowel + /r/ of Spanish *carta* 'map'.

3. /ɔ/, /ou/ and /ɔː/ (if there is no letter *r* in the spelling) are all confused, a vowel intermediate between /ɔ/ and /ɔː/ being used for all three. Where *r* occurs in the spelling /ɔː/ is replaced by the vowel + /r/ of Spanish *porque* 'because'.

4. /uː/ and /u/ are confused, the replacement being a vowel usually more like /uː/ than /u/.

5. /əː/ is replaced by the vowel + /r/ of Spanish *ser* 'be'.

6. /ə/ is usually replaced by some other vowel suggested by the spelling (with /r/ added if the spelling has *r*).

7. /iə, ɛə, uə/ are replaced by the vowel + /r/ of Spanish *ir* 'go', *ser* 'be', *duro* 'hard'.

8. There is no distinction between long and short vowels in Spanish, and all vowels have the same length as the English short vowels. Special attention must be given to lengthening the long vowels.

Rhythm in Spanish is like that of French or Hindi. Stressed syllables occur, but each syllable has approximately the same length and there is none of the variation in length which results in English from the grouping of syllables into rhythm units. Special attention must be given to this, to the use of /ə/ in weak syllables and to the weak forms of unstressed words, which do not occur in Spanish.

APPENDIX 2
USEFUL BOOKS AND RECORDINGS

SOME USEFUL BOOKS FOR FURTHER STUDY

Textbooks

Gimson, A. C. *An Introduction to the Pronunciation of English.* Edward Arnold.

Jones, D. *An Outline of English Phonetics.* Cambridge University Press.

Jones, D. *English Pronouncing Dictionary.* Dent.

Lado, R. and Fries, C. C. *English Pronunciation.* University of Michigan Press.

O'Connor, J. D. and Arnold, G. F. *Intonation of Colloquial English.* Longman.

Pring, J. T. *Colloquial English Pronunciation.* Longman.

Practice Books

Arnold, G. F. and Gimson, A. C. *English Pronunciation Practice.* Hodder.

Barnard, G. L. and McKay, P. S. *Practice in Spoken English.* Macmillan.

Hill, L. A. *Drills and Tests in English Sounds.* Longman.

Trim, John, *English Pronunciation Illustrated.* Cambridge University Press.

USEFUL BOOKS AND RECORDINGS

Phonetic readers (with intonation marking)

MacCarthy, P. A. D. *English Conversation Reader*. Longman.

O'Connor, J. D. *Phonetic Drill Reader*. Cambridge University Press.

O'Connor, J. D. *Advanced Phonetic Reader*. Cambridge University Press.

GRAMOPHONE RECORDS

O'Connor, J. D. *A Course of English Pronunciation*. B.B.C.

O'Connor, J. D. *English Intonation*. B.B.C.

CASSETTE RECORDINGS

O'Connor, J. D. *Better English Pronunciation*. Cambridge University Press.

O'Connor, J. D. *Phonetic Drill Reader*. Cambridge University Press.

O'Connor, J. D. *Advanced Phonetic Reader*. Cambridge University Press.

Trim, John, *English Pronunciation Illustrated*. Cambridge University Press.

Recordings for use with the above four books are available; please refer to the current Cambridge University Press catalogue for details.